p43 cherry cake

Gooseberry Patch Co.

A Country Store In Your Mailbox®

Country Baking

A Country Store In Your Mailbox®

Gooseberry Patch
600 London Road
Department Book
Delaware, OH 43015

1·800·854·6673
www.gooseberrypatch.com

Copyright 2000, Gooseberry Patch 1-888052-73-2
Seventh Printing, December, 2004

Do you have a tried & true recipe...

tip, craft or memory that you'd like to see featured in a **Gooseberry Patch** book? Visit our web site at **www.gooseberrypatch.com**, register and follow the easy steps to submit your favorite family recipe.
Or send them to us at:

Gooseberry Patch
Attn: Book Dept.
P.O. Box 190
Delaware, OH 43015

Don't forget to include the number of servings your recipe makes, plus your name, street address, phone number and e-mail address. If we select your recipe, your name will appear right along with it...and you'll receive a **FREE** copy of the book!

Contents

Dedication

To all our friends who find delight in freshly-baked pies, fluffy buttermilk biscuits and old-fashioned layer cakes!

Appreciation

Heartfelt appreciation to all who shared their cherished favorites.

Biscuits & Rolls

Bride's Biscuits

Becky Sykes
Gooseberry Patch

I have an old recipe file that I keep all my favorites in. This is a recipe our family loves with homemade jelly or served alongside ham.

3-1/2 c. all-purpose flour,
   divided
2 t. baking powder
1/4 t. salt
1 T. sugar

1/2 c. shortening
1 pkg. active dry yeast
1/3 c. warm water
3/4 c. milk

In a medium bowl, combine 3 cups flour, baking powder, salt and sugar. Cut in shortening to resemble coarse crumbs. Soften yeast in warm water. Stir yeast and milk into flour mixture. Sprinkle a board with remaining flour. Turn out dough and knead several times; pat out to 1/2-inch thickness. Cut dough with a floured biscuit cutter and place biscuits one inch apart on lightly greased baking sheets. Prick dough several times with a fork. Set aside in a warm place for 20 minutes. Bake at 450 degrees for 8 to 10 minutes or until biscuits are golden. Cool on racks. Makes 1-1/2 dozen.

A pretty hatbox is the perfect gift for a new bride. She can fill it with all the sentimental reminders and cherished photographs of her wedding day.

Old-Fashioned Potato Rolls

Geneva Rogers
Gillette, WY

Soft, delicious rolls, great for dinner or split for sandwiches.

1 pkg. active dry yeast
3 T. sugar, divided
1/3 c. warm water
1 c. potatoes, cooked and
    mashed
2/3 c. sour cream

1/4 c. butter, melted and cooled
2 t. salt
2 eggs
4 to 4-1/2 c. all-purpose flour
2 T. butter, melted

Combine yeast and one tablespoon sugar in warm water; stir until yeast is dissolved and foamy, 5 to 10 minutes. Mix together mashed potatoes, sour cream, 1/4 cup butter, remaining sugar, salt and eggs; stir into yeast mixture and spoon into the bowl of a heavy-duty mixer. On low speed, beat in flour, 1/2 cup at a time, until a stiff dough forms. Place dough on a lightly floured surface and knead 5 to 10 minutes. Place dough in a large greased bowl, turning to coat top. Loosely cover with a cloth and let rise until double in size, about one hour. Punch down dough and roll into a long rope; cut rope in 12 equal pieces. Roll each piece into a ball and place balls of dough in a greased 13"x9" baking pan. Brush tops of rolls with remaining melted butter, cover and let rise 45 minutes. Bake at 375 degrees for 20 minutes or until golden. Makes one dozen rolls.

My idea of heaven is a great big baked potato and someone to share it with.

-Oprah Winfrey

7

Dixie's Sky High Biscuits

Diane Christensen
Tremonton, UT

Serve these with homemade sausage gravy!

3 c. all-purpose flour
4-1/2 t. baking powder
3/4 t. cream of tartar
2 T. sugar

1/2 t. salt
3/4 c. butter
1 egg, beaten
1 c. milk

Combine flour, baking powder, cream of tartar, sugar and salt. Cut in butter until mixture is coarse and crumbly. Add egg and milk, stirring quickly until just mixed. On lightly floured board, knead briefly. Roll to about one-inch thickness. Cut the dough with a round biscuit cutter. Place on a greased cookie sheet. Bake at 400 degrees for 12 to 15 minutes.

Onion Dinner Rolls

Anna McMaster
Portland, OR

Easy to make rolls with a hint of onion and dill.

1 stick butter, melted
1-1/2 t. dried parsley
1/2 t. dill weed

1 T. dried onion flakes
2 T. grated Parmesan cheese
10-oz. tube buttermilk biscuits

Place butter in a bowl and stir in parsley, dill weed, onion flakes and cheese. Separate biscuits and cut into fourths, dip in butter mixture, coating all sides. Place biscuits in a greased 9"x9" baking dish and bake at 425 degrees for 15 minutes.

A collection of butter and salt crocks along a pine shelf creates a nostalgic feel in your kitchen.

Alabama Biscuits

Jean Shaffer
Washington Court House, OH

*Call several friends and invite them over for a casual
mid-morning brunch; it's a nice way to catch up.*

3 c. all-purpose flour	1 c. milk
2 T. sugar	1 pkg. active dry yeast
2 t. baking powder	1/3 c. warm water
1 t. salt	1/4 c. butter, melted
4 T. shortening	

Sift together flour, sugar, baking powder and salt. Heat shortening and milk in a saucepan until shortening melts. In small bowl, mix together yeast and warm water. Mix liquids together and add to flour mixture. On a floured board, roll out dough to 1/2-inch thick. Cut 20 biscuits with a biscuit cutter, place 10 on a greased baking sheet. Brush biscuits with melted butter, top each with another biscuit. Let rise until double in size. Bake at 425 degrees for 15 minutes.

Tell a friend no one else can fill her shoes!
Use glue to cover a shoe box with pictures of shoes you've
cut out of catalogs. Let dry, then place your biscuits
and a jar of jam inside the box.

Homemade Dinner Rolls

Pamela Christopher
Pulaski, TN

Homemade taste that's just perfect for a Sunday dinner.

1 c. boiling water
1 c. sugar
1 c. shortening
1-1/2 t. salt

1 c. lukewarm water
2 pkgs. active dry yeast
3 eggs, beaten
6 c. all-purpose flour

In medium bowl, mix together boiling water, sugar, shortening and salt. In separate bowl, blend lukewarm water and yeast together. Combine sugar mixture and yeast mixture; blend in eggs. Add flour, stir and refrigerate overnight. On a lightly floured surface, roll out dough, cut with a biscuit cutter and place on a lightly oiled baking sheet; allow to rise in a warm place for one to 2 hours. Bake at 375 degrees for 15 to 20 minutes or until tops are lightly browned.

Sweet Cream Biscuits

Stephanie Moon
Boise, ID

Top with fresh berry preserves.

2 c. all-purpose flour
1 T. baking powder
1/2 c. powdered sugar
1/2 t. cream of tartar

1/4 t. salt
1/2 c. butter
2/3 c. half-and-half

Stir together flour, baking powder, sugar, cream of tartar and salt. Cut in butter until mixture resembles coarse crumbs. Make a well in the center of dry ingredients and stir in half-and-half. Drop dough by heaping spoonfuls onto ungreased baking sheet. Bake at 450 degrees for 8 to 10 minutes or until light golden brown. Makes one dozen biscuits.

Grow old along with me, the best is yet to be.

-Robert Browning

Easy Refrigerator Rolls

Zoe Bennett
Columbia, SC

Delicious rolls that taste like Grandma's.

2 c. warm water
2 pkgs. active dry yeast
1/2 c. sugar
1/4 c. oil

1 t. salt
1 egg, beaten
7 c. all-purpose flour

Blend together warm water, yeast, sugar, oil and salt; stir in egg and flour. Mix well and place in a greased bowl, turning once to coat. Loosely cover with a cloth and let rise in a warm place until double in bulk. Punch down dough, cover and refrigerate until ready to use; dough will stay fresh for one to 2 weeks. When making rolls, shape into one-inch balls, placing 3 balls in each section of a buttered muffin tin; let rise until double. Bake at 400 degrees for 15 to 20 minutes or until golden. Makes approximately 3 dozen rolls.

A new daughter-in-law would love to receive copies of your time-tested family recipes! Look for antique recipe cards at flea markets and jot down some of your favorites. Surprise her by placing them in an old-fashioned recipe file.

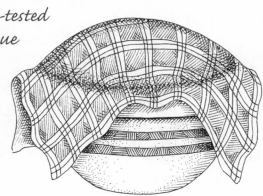

Pumpkin Biscuits

Sandy Peterson
Glen Ellyn, IL

Biscuits with a beautiful color and a spicy taste.

2 c. all-purpose flour
4 T. sugar, divided
1 T. baking powder
1 t. baking soda
1/4 t. salt
1/4 t. cinnamon

1/4 t. nutmeg
1/4 t. allspice
1/2 c. butter, chilled
2/3 c. canned pumpkin
1/2 c. buttermilk

Sift together flour, 2 tablespoons sugar and next 6 ingredients in a large bowl. Cut in the butter until mixture resembles coarse crumbs. In a small bowl, whisk together pumpkin and buttermilk. Add to flour mixture and stir to combine. Knead gently a few times. Roll out dough to 1/2-inch thickness and cut using a biscuit or cookie cutter. Place biscuits on lightly greased cookie sheet and sprinkle tops with remaining sugar. Bake 10 minutes at 450 degrees, watching carefully until they're lightly golden; don't let brown. Makes 12 to 18 biscuits.

Little ones will love these pumpkin biscuits as a snack! Use a marker to draw a Jack-o'-Lantern face on tiny orange gift sacks. Put a biscuit in each sack and tie closed with green curling ribbon.

Ginger-Molasses Biscuits

*Kelly Alderson
Erie, PA*

Try these topped with apple butter!

1 stick unsalted butter, softened
1/3 c. brown sugar, packed
2 T. molasses
1/4 c. apple cider
1 T. ginger

2 c. all-purpose flour
1/2 t. baking soda
1/2 c. crystallized ginger, finely
    minced

Cream butter and sugar; stir in molasses and apple cider. In a separate bowl, combine ginger, flour, baking soda and candied ginger; stir into butter mixture. Cover dough with plastic wrap and refrigerate one hour. Roll out dough 3/4-inch thick and cut into rounds with a 2-inch glass dipped in sugar. Bake at 350 degrees on a lightly oiled cookie sheet for 12 to 15 minutes.

A basket of still-warm biscuits makes a perfect gift if you're sharing a special meal such as Thanksgiving dinner.

Melt-Away Biscuits

Karen Thomas
Princess Anne, MD

Simple to make, they melt in your mouth!

1 c. butter, melted   2 c. self-rising flour
1 c. sour cream

Blend butter and sour cream together; mix in flour. Fill lightly oiled muffin tins 2/3 full with batter. Bake at 350 degrees for 30 minutes. Makes 12 to 14 biscuits.

Easy Cinnamon Rolls

Robyn Wright
Delaware, OH

Wrap the ingredients separately, add the recipe and tuck in a gathering basket; a wonderful treat for a new friend.

2 c. biscuit baking mix   1/4 c. sugar
2/3 c. milk   1 t. cinnamon
1/8 c. butter, softened

Mix biscuit baking mix and milk in a small bowl with a fork. Knead dough gently 8 to 10 times on lightly floured surface. Roll into a 12"x7" rectangle; spread thinly with butter. In a separate small bowl, mix sugar and cinnamon. Sprinkle dough with sugar mixture. Roll up tightly, starting with long end; pinch edges to seal. Cut into one-inch slices and put one slice in each cup of a lightly oiled muffin tin. Bake at 425 degrees for 15 minutes or until rolls are lightly golden. Makes approximately one dozen.

Buttermilk Biscuits

The Governor's Inn
Ludlow, VT

We serve these feather-light biscuits with dinner each night.

2-1/2 c. all-purpose flour
3 T. sugar
1-1/2 T. baking powder

1/4 t. salt
1/2 c. unsalted butter, softened
1 c. buttermilk

Combine flour, sugar, baking powder and salt in a mixing bowl; blend well. Add butter, stir in buttermilk until just mixed; do not overwork. Spoon batter into greased muffin tins and bake at 350 degrees for 30 minutes. Turn out and serve warm. Makes 12 to 18 biscuits.

Take time to enjoy a hearty family breakfast... warm biscuits with homemade jam, flapjacks with maple syrup, crisp bacon, sausage and farm-fresh eggs!

Heart-Shaped Dill Rolls

Penny Sherman
Cumming, GA

I love to serve these on Valentine's day and for bridal showers.

3 pkgs. active dry yeast
2/3 c. warm water
1/4 c. sugar
2-1/2 c. small curd cottage
    cheese
1 t. salt
1-1/2 oz. pkg. dry onion
    soup mix

3 T. butter
1 T. fresh parsley, minced
3 t. dill seeds
3 eggs
1/2 t. baking soda
7 c. all-purpose flour

Stir yeast into warm water until thoroughly dissolved. In a medium saucepan, blend together next 7 ingredients, heating until just warm. Remove saucepan from heat and beat in yeast mixture, eggs and baking soda with a heavy-duty mixer. Blend in enough flour to form a stiff dough. Using dough hook on mixer, knead dough until smooth. Place in a greased bowl, turn to coat and let rise until double in size. Punch down and roll out to 1/2-inch thickness on a lightly floured board. Cut dough with a floured heart-shaped cookie cutter. Place rolls on a greased baking sheet; let rise until double. Bake at 400 degrees for 15 to 20 minutes. Makes 5 dozen rolls.

Perfect for a bridal shower luncheon...heart-shaped rolls filled with chicken salad and topped with organic pansies or violas.

Sweet Potato Biscuits

Ruth Gomez
Toledo, Ohio

These taste great!

3/4 c. sweet potatoes, cooked,
    peeled, mashed and chilled
1 stick butter, melted and cooled
1/4 c. brown sugar, packed

1/2 c. milk
2 c. all-purpose flour
1/2 t. salt
1-1/2 t. baking powder

In a large bowl, combine the sweet potatoes, butter and brown sugar. Stir in the milk and blend until smooth. Sift together dry ingredients and add to sweet potato mixture. Turn dough onto a lightly floured counter and knead 2 minutes. With floured rolling pin, roll dough until 1/2-inch thick. Cut out with a 2-inch round cutter. Place biscuits one inch apart on a lightly greased cookie sheet. Bake at 400 degrees for 15 minutes or until light brown. Makes about 1-1/2 dozen biscuits.

Anyone would be thrilled to receive yummy biscuits
or rolls in a basket lined with a pretty bread cloth.
Just stitch buttons of different sizes and colors along the edges
of a homespun napkin; line your basket and fill!

Corn & Bacon Biscuits

Robin Hill
Rochester, NY

Slice and serve with a bowl of bean soup, or warm them
up the next morning to serve with breakfast.

8 bacon slices, crisply cooked
   and crumbled, drippings
   reserved
2 c. all-purpose flour
1 c. cornmeal
3 T. sugar
5 t. baking powder

1-1/4 t. salt
1/2 c. plus 2 T. unsalted butter,
   chilled and cut into pieces
2 eggs, beaten
6 T. buttermilk
1-3/4 t. dried sage
1 c. corn

Prepare bacon; set aside. Combine flour, cornmeal, sugar, baking powder and salt in a large bowl. Cut in butter until mixture resembles coarse meal. Blend together eggs, buttermilk, sage and 2 tablespoons reserved bacon drippings. Stir into flour mixture to form a soft dough; add corn and bacon. Place dough on a lightly floured surface and knead one minute. Roll dough into a one-inch thick, 10"x8" rectangle. Cut rectangle into 12 equal squares; place squares on an oiled baking sheet. Bake at 375 degrees for 25 minutes or until golden.

When the weather gets cool and crisp, it's the perfect time to host a bean supper! A simmering pot of bean soup, cornbread and biscuits are perfect together!

Cottage Cheese Rolls

Carol Sheets
Delaware, OH

These are very easy to make and have a delicious light flavor.

2 pkgs. active dry yeast
1/2 c. lukewarm water
2 c. small curd cottage cheese
1/4 c. sugar
2 t. salt

1/2 t. baking soda
2 eggs
4-1/2 c. all-purpose flour,
    divided

Sprinkle yeast in lukewarm water; stir to dissolve. Heat cottage cheese in a saucepan until just warm. Spoon into a large mixing bowl and combine with sugar, salt, baking soda, eggs and one cup of flour. Beat with an electric mixer at medium speed until smooth, about 2 minutes, scraping the sides of the bowl occasionally. Gradually add enough of the remaining flour to form a soft dough that doesn't stick to the sides of the bowl. Place dough in a greased bowl, turning once to coat. Loosely cover with a cloth and let rise in a warm place until double in size, about 1-1/2 hours. Turn dough onto a lightly floured surface and divide into 24 equal pieces. Shape each piece of dough into a ball and place 12 balls in 2 greased 9" round baking pans. Let dough rise again until double in size, about 45 minutes. Bake at 350 degrees for 20 minutes or until golden. Remove from pans and cool on racks. Brush tops with melted butter if desired.

Choose thy friends like thy books, few but choice.

-James Howell

Hearty Maple Biscuits

John Alexander
New Britain, CT

Quick and easy; great for breakfast on a chilly morning!

1/2 c. maple syrup
2 T. butter
8-oz. tube refrigerated
    buttermilk biscuits

2 T. orange juice
1/2 c. nuts, finely chopped

Blend together syrup and butter; pour in an ungreased 8"x8" pan. Place pan in a 400 degree oven until butter melts. Remove from oven and stir to blend syrup and butter. Separate biscuit dough and dip in orange juice; roll in nuts. Lay biscuits in pan over syrup and butter. Bake at 400 degrees for 15 to 20 minutes. Makes 10 biscuits.

Cinnamon Spread

Marian Buckley
Fontana, CA

Serve this wonderful spread over still-warm rolls or biscuits.

1/2 c. butter, softened
3/4 c. sugar

1 T. cinnamon

Combine all ingredients; beating until smooth and creamy.

Overnight Cinnamon-Pecan Buns

_No_ (written above "Overnight")

Joan Groover
Media, PA

A delicious recipe; it doesn't get any easier than this to prepare wonderful cinnamon buns! There's nothing better than having company for a weekend and waking them up to the sweet smell of cinnamon...just don't tell them how easy the recipe is!

1 c. raisins
1 c. pecans
48-oz. pkg. frozen dinner rolls
3-1/2 oz. pkg. non-instant
    butterscotch pudding mix

1/2 c. brown sugar, packed
1/2 c. sugar
2 t. cinnamon
1/2 c. butter, melted

In the bottom of a 13"x9" baking dish, evenly spread raisins and pecans; top with frozen dinner rolls. Mix dry butterscotch pudding with brown sugar and sprinkle over rolls. Stir together sugar and cinnamon and sprinkle over all. Pour melted butter evenly over the top of all ingredients and set in oven to rise, covered with plastic wrap, overnight. When ready to serve, uncover and return pan to oven. Set oven at 350 degrees and leave rolls in oven while temperature is rising. When oven temperature reaches 350 degrees set timer for 40 to 50 minutes and bake buns until bottoms are golden.

Make a fragrant kitchen garland for over a door or mantel... string whole nutmegs, cinnamon sticks, bay leaves and tiny nutmeg graters on heavy jute.

Vanilla Sweet Rolls

Carrie O'Shea
Marina Del Ray, CA

An easy recipe the kids will enjoy helping with.

2 pkgs. active dry yeast
1 c. warm water
3-1/2 oz. pkg. instant vanilla
  pudding mix

1/4 c. oil
1/2 t. salt
2 to 3 c. all-purpose flour

Sprinkle yeast over warm water; stir to dissolve. Add dry pudding, oil and salt until well blended. Stir in enough flour until dough is no longer sticky. Place dough on a lightly floured board and knead until smooth. Roll dough out to 1/2-inch thick and cut with a 2-inch round biscuit or cookie cutter. Place rolls on an oiled baking sheet and let rise one hour. Bake at 400 degrees for 10 minutes. Makes approximately 18 rolls.

Homemade vanilla sugar is great for sprinkling on toast or hot cereal. Just combine 4 cups sugar with 1/4 cup cinnamon. Cut a whole vanilla bean into one-inch pieces. Blend together and store in an airtight container for 2 weeks. Remove the vanilla bean before using.

Brown Sugar Drop Biscuits

Kathy Grashoff
Ft. Wayne, IN

Filled with brown sugar, these drop biscuits are so simple to make!

1-1/2 c. plus 2 T. all-purpose
    flour, divided
1/2 c. whole wheat flour
2 t. baking powder
1 t. baking soda
1/2 t. salt

1 stick butter, chilled and cut
    into pieces
3/4 c. apple juice
1 T. cinnamon
2 T. butter, softened
1/2 c. brown sugar, packed

Sift together 1-1/2 cups all-purpose flour, whole wheat flour, baking powder, baking soda and salt in medium bowl. With pastry blender or your hands, cut in butter until mixture is crumbly. Stir in enough apple juice to form a dough that's just moist enough to drop from a spoon. For topping, stir together cinnamon, remaining flour, butter and brown sugar in small bowl until well mixed. To form each biscuit, drop a generous teaspoon of dough onto a lightly oiled baking sheet. Crumble about 1/2 teaspoon of the topping into the center. Top with another teaspoon of the dough, followed by a final 1/2 teaspoon of topping. Continue dropping biscuits, about 2 inches apart. Bake biscuits in a 400 degree oven 10 minutes or until flaky and lightly browned. Makes about 20 biscuits.

Call a friend today who you haven't seen in awhile!

Cheesy Colorado Biscuits

Rhonda Reeder
Ellicott City, MD

*We enjoyed these many times while visiting family in
Colorado. They're perfect with a bowl of chili!*

1/2 c. margarine, softened
5-oz. jar pasteurized process
   cheese spread

1 c. all-purpose flour
1 to 2 drops hot pepper sauce

Blend together margarine and cheese until smooth. Stir in flour and
hot sauce, mixing well. Shape into 1-1/2 inch balls and place on an
ungreased cookie sheet; press flat with the back of a fork. Bake at
350 degrees for 10 minutes.

Bacon Crunch Drop Biscuits

April Jacobs
Loveland, CO

Fast to make and so flaky!

1/2 c. bacon, crisply cooked and
   crumbled
2 c. self-rising flour

1/4 t. baking soda
1/4 c. oil
3/4 c. buttermilk

Prepare bacon; set aside. Sift together flour and baking soda. Blend oil
and buttermilk; add to flour mixture. Stir in bacon and drop by spoonfuls onto a lightly oiled baking sheet. Bake at 425 degrees for 10 to
15 minutes or golden brown. Makes one dozen biscuits.

*Give someone special a coupon book!
Include free leaf raking,
a night of babysitting or an
afternoon of garden weeding.*

Bran Yeast Rolls

Jeannie Craig
Charlotte, NC

Nothing makes the house smell better than homemade bread.
My family loves it when the urge strikes me to bake!

1-1/2 c. shortening	3 eggs, beaten
3/4 c. sugar	3 pkgs. active dry yeast
2 t. salt	1-1/2 c. warm water
1-1/2 c. boiling water	8 c. all-purpose flour
1-1/2 c. bran cereal	1-1/2 c. butter, melted

Cream shortening, sugar and salt at medium speed of electric mixer
until well blended. Add boiling water; mix well. Stir in cereal and eggs.
Dissolve yeast in warm water, add to shortening mixture, stirring well.
Mix in one cup of flour, then, using a dough hook on heavy-duty
mixer, gradually add enough remaining flour to make a soft dough.
Place in a greased bowl, turning once to coat top. Cover and let rise in
warm place, free from drafts for one hour. Divide dough in half, roll
out, cut into circles. Dip each circle in butter, fold over and place close
together on lightly oiled baking sheet. Cover with light towel and
let rise one hour. Bake at 400 degrees for 8 minutes or until
lightly brown.

The smell of coffee cooking
was a reason for growing up,
because children were never allowed
to have it and nothing haunted the
nostrils all the way out to the
barn as did the aroma
of boiling coffee.

- Edna Lewis

Sour Cream Quick Rolls

Kay Lowe
Tomball, TX

With only 3 ingredients, these couldn't be easier!

2-1/4 c. biscuit baking mix, divided

8 oz. sour cream
1/2 c. butter, melted

In a large bowl, combine 2 cups biscuit mix, sour cream and butter. Stir well. Sprinkle remaining 1/4 cup biscuit mix on a flat surface, breaking up any large lumps. Drop batter by level tablespoons onto biscuit mix and roll into 36 balls. Place 3 balls into each cup of a greased 12-cup muffin tin. Bake at 350 degrees for 20 to 25 minutes, or until golden brown. Makes one dozen.

Sweet Cheese Rolls

Kathy Grashoff
Ft. Wayne, IN

Yummy rolls with a cream cheese filling!

3/4 c. sugar
1/4 c. pecans, chopped
1 T. orange zest
2 3-oz. pkgs. cream cheese, softened

2 10-oz. tubes refrigerated flaky biscuits
1/2 c. butter, melted

Combine sugar, pecans and zest; set aside. Cut cream cheese into 20 equal pieces. Separate each biscuit into 2 layers and place one piece of cream cheese between layers; seal edges. Dip each filled biscuit into butter, then into sugar mixture. Place on ungreased cookie sheet and bake at 350 degrees for 15 to 20 minutes or until browned. Makes 20 rolls.

Friendship is a sheltering tree.

-Samuel Taylor Coleridge

Grandma Lux's Rolls

Donna Cozzens
Laramie, WY

These are incredible!

2 pkgs. active dry yeast	1 c. boiling water
1-1/2 c. warm water, divided	1 t. salt
2 sticks butter	3 eggs
3/4 c. sugar	8 c. all-purpose flour

Dissolve yeast in 1/2 cup warm water; set aside. Mix butter, sugar and boiling water until dissolved; add salt. Beat the eggs and stir into butter mixture; add yeast mixture. Stir in flour alternately with remaining cup warm water. The dough should pull away from the sides of the bowl when ready. Place the dough in large greased bowl; grease top of dough and cover with plastic wrap. Allow dough to sit in refrigerator at least 18 hours. Remove the dough from the refrigerator and allow it to stand for one hour. Shape dough into balls about half the size of a baseball. Place on greased baking sheet and allow dough to rise for an hour or until double. Bake at 350 degrees for 20 minutes. Makes approximately 3 to 4 dozen rolls.

Spice a dish with love and it pleases every palate.

-Plautus

Nutty Applesauce Biscuits

Diana Chaney
Olathe, KS

Biscuits with a sweet praline taste!

1/2 c. butter, chilled and cut into
    12 pieces
1/2 c. brown sugar, packed
36 pecan halves

cinnamon to taste
2 c. biscuit baking mix
1/3 c. applesauce
1/3 c. milk

Arrange one slice of butter, 2 teaspoons of the brown sugar and 3 of the pecan halves in each of 12 greased muffin cups; sprinkle with cinnamon. Heat in a 400 degree oven until the butter and sugar dissolve. Combine the baking mix, applesauce and milk in a medium mixing bowl and stir by hand 20 strokes. Drop by spoonfuls over the butter mixture in the prepared muffin cups. Bake at 400 degrees for 10 minutes or until golden brown. Invert onto a serving platter immediately. Makes 12 biscuits.

Fill a small apple basket with raffia and colorful autumn leaves. Wrap your nutty applesauce biscuits in tissue and set inside. Make a gift tag by writing on an autumn leaf with a gold pen. . . a thoughtful and colorful hostess gift!

Butterscotch Rolls

Julie DeGroote
Urbana, IL

The combination of butterscotch and coconut is really good.

1 pkg. active dry yeast
1/4 c. warm water
3-1/2 oz. pkg. non-instant
    butterscotch pudding mix
1-1/2 c. plus 2 T. evaporated
    milk, divided
1/2 c. plus 2 T. butter, divided
2 eggs
2 t. salt

4-1/2 to 5 c. plus 2 T.
    all-purpose flour, divided
1/4 c. butter, melted
2/3 c. flaked coconut
2/3 c. plus 1/4 c. brown sugar,
    packed and divided
1/3 c. nuts, chopped
1 c. powdered sugar

Soften yeast in warm water; set aside. Prepare dry pudding according to package directions using 1-1/2 cups evaporated milk. When pudding is thick, remove from heat and add 1/2 cup butter. Stir and cool to lukewarm. Blend in 2 eggs, salt and yeast. Gradually add 4-1/2 to 5 cups flour; beating well after each addition. Cover and let rise until light and double in size, about 1-1/2 hours. In separate bowl, blend together 2 tablespoons butter, coconut, 2/3 cup brown sugar, nuts and remaining flour. Roll out dough to 1/2-inch thick and top with coconut mixture. Roll dough jelly roll-style and slice into one-inch rounds. Place rolls in 2 lightly oiled 9"x9" pans; let rise until double. Bake at 350 degrees for 15 to 20 minutes or until done. Combine remaining brown sugar, evaporated milk and melted butter in a saucepan. Boil for one minute. Blend in powdered sugar and drizzle on warm rolls.

Basically the only thing we need is a hand
that rests on our own, that wishes it well,
that sometimes guides us.

-Hector Bianciotti

Amish Orange Rolls

Angela Murphy
Tempe, AZ

This recipe was found in a very old Amish cookbook.

1 c. shortening	1 c. warm water
2/3 c. sugar	1/2 c. orange juice
1 T. salt	4 T. orange zest
2 c. milk, scalded	4 eggs, beaten
3 T. active dry yeast	11 to 14 c. all-purpose flour

Cream together shortening, sugar, salt and milk; set aside to cool. Dissolve yeast in warm water then stir into cooled milk mixture. Add orange juice, orange zest, eggs and yeast mixture. Using a heavy-duty mixer or by hand, stir in 8 cups of flour. Place on a lightly floured board and knead in enough remaining flour until dough is smooth and elastic. Place in greased bowl, turn dough to coat and let rise until double in size. Roll out 3/4-inch thick and cut with a biscuit cutter. Place in oiled 13"x9" baking pans or on cookie sheets, about one inch apart, and let rise again until double. Bake at 325 degrees for 20 to 25 minutes. Cool before icing.

Orange Icing:

4 T. orange juice	3 c. powdered sugar
1 T. orange zest	

Combine ingredients well and drizzle over warm orange rolls.

Glazed Spice Biscuits

Cheri Maxwell
Gulf Breeze, FL

A moist and spicy biscuit I like to serve with a mug of warm cider.

2-1/4 c. all-purpose flour
4 t. baking powder
1 t. ginger
1 t. cinnamon
3/4 t. salt
1/2 t. cardamom
1/2 c. unsalted butter, chilled
    and cut into pieces
1/2 c. canned pumpkin
1/4 c. plus 2 T. whipping cream,
    chilled and divided
1/3 c. brown sugar, packed
4 T. honey, divided
1 t. lemon zest
1/2 c. walnuts, chopped
16 walnut halves

Sift together flour, baking powder, ginger, cinnamon, salt and cardamom. Cut in butter until mixture resembles coarse crumbs. In a separate bowl blend together pumpkin, 1/4 cup cream, brown sugar, 2 tablespoons honey and zest. Stir walnuts into pumpkin mixture and stir into dry ingredients. On a lightly floured surface, knead dough until smooth. Roll out to 3/4-inch thickness and cut biscuits using a 2-inch biscuit cutter; place on an oiled baking sheet. Blend together remaining cream and honey; brush over biscuits. Top each biscuit with a walnut half. Bake at 375 degrees for 20 to 25 minutes.

Enjoy a special lunch just for two. On a golden autumn day, pack a bicycle basket with a cozy fleece blanket, thermos of homemade soup and some warm rolls, then take a bike ride in the country with a special friend!

Garlic Biscuits

Judy Kelly
St. Charles, MO

We think they're perfect with any meal or even for a snack.

2 c. biscuit baking mix
1/2 c. Cheddar cheese, finely
    shredded

2/3 c. milk
1/4 c. butter
1/4 t. garlic powder

Mix biscuit baking mix, Cheddar cheese and milk until blended. Drop by tablespoonfuls on greased or parchment-lined cookie sheets. Bake at 450 degrees for 10 minutes. Melt butter and garlic powder together and pour over hot biscuits.

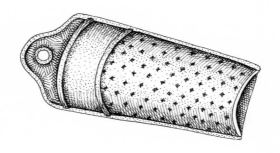

Mini-Sausage Biscuits

Susie Backus
Gooseberry Patch

You can use mild or sage sausage if you'd like to change the flavor.

2-1/4 c. biscuit baking mix
2/3 c. milk
1 lb. bulk sausage, browned and
    drained

2 c. sharp Cheddar cheese,
    grated

Combine ingredients. Knead on a floured surface and roll out to 1/2-inch thick. Form into one-inch balls and bake at 350 degrees for 20 minutes.

Freckled Rolls

Tiffany Brinkley
Broomfield, CO

An old family recipe that's been handed down for years. We've never known how it came by this fun name, but it makes the kids giggle!

1 pkg. active dry yeast
1-1/2 c. warm water, divided
1/2 c. sugar
1/3 c. dry milk
1/2 c. butter, softened

1-1/2 t. salt
1 c. wheat bran
6-1/4 to 6-3/4 c. bread flour,
    divided
3 eggs, beaten

Combine yeast with 1/4 cup warm water; stir until yeast is dissolved. Blend in remaining water, sugar, dry milk, butter, salt, wheat bran and 2 cups flour. Using a heavy-duty mixer, beat dough 2 minutes at medium speed. Add eggs and one cup flour; beat 2 minutes at high speed. Blend in enough remaining flour until a soft dough forms. On a lightly floured surface or with paddle attachment on mixer, knead dough until smooth, 8 to 10 minutes. Place dough in a lightly oiled bowl, turn to coat top. Cover bowl with plastic wrap and refrigerate for 2 hours. When double in size, remove from refrigerator; punch down. Shape into 2-inch balls and place close together on an oiled cookie sheet. Bake at 425 degrees for 12 to 15 minutes. Makes approximately 3 dozen rolls.

The best thing to give a friend is your heart.

-Francis Maitland Balfour

Cheddar Cheese Biscuits

Audrey Lett
Newark, DE

Fresh dill and chives make these rolls perfect for serving whenever we grill out, or even split and topped with homemade chicken salad!

3 c. all-purpose flour
4-1/2 t. baking powder
1 T. sugar
1-1/2 t. dry mustard
1 t. salt
1/2 stick unsalted butter, chilled
   and cut into pieces
1/4 c. shortening, chilled and cut
   into pieces
1 c. plus 2 T. milk
1/4 c. fresh chives, chopped
3 T. fresh dill, chopped
2-1/2 c. sharp Cheddar cheese,
   grated and divided

Sift together flour, baking powder, sugar, mustard and salt. Cut in butter and shortening until crumbly. Blend together milk, chives and dill, stir into dry ingredients and add in 2 cups cheese. On a lightly floured surface, knead dough lightly. Roll out 1/2-inch thick and cut using a floured biscuit cutter. Sprinkle biscuit tops with remaining cheese, place on a lightly oiled baking sheet and bake at 450 degrees for 15 minutes. Makes approximately 18 biscuits.

Not all biscuits have to be round! Use your cookie cutters to create fun whimsical shapes...acorns, snowmen, sunflowers, gingerbread men or snowflakes.

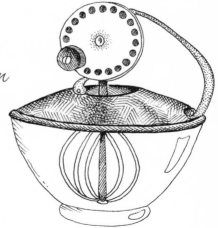

Quick Breads, Muffins & Coffee Cakes

Sour Cream-Cinnamon Coffee Cake

Karen Moran
Navasota, TX

Whenever we have guests, I serve this moist coffee cake for breakfast. It's a recipe I know I can always count on.

1-3/4 c. sugar, divided
2 sticks butter
2 eggs
1/2 pt. sour cream
2 c. all-purpose flour

1/2 t. baking soda
1-1/2 t. baking powder
1 t. vanilla extract
1 c. nuts, chopped
2 t. cinnamon

Combine 1-1/4 cups sugar, butter and eggs in mixer. Beat until fluffy and blend in sour cream. Sift together flour, baking soda and baking powder; add to creamed mixture. Add vanilla and blend well. Spoon 1/2 of mixture into greased and floured 10" tube pan. Mix nuts, cinnamon and remaining sugar together in small bowl. Sprinkle 1/2 of the nut mixture over batter. Spoon on remaining batter, sprinkle on remaining nut mixture. Bake for one hour at 350 degrees.

The torch of love is lit in the kitchen.

-French proverb

Blueberry & Lemon Muffins

Beth Blythe
St. Clair, MI

When I was a child, Mom and I would go blueberry picking
then hurry home to make these delicious muffins!

1-3/4 c. all-purpose flour
1/2 c. plus 2 T. sugar, divided
2-1/2 t. baking powder
3/4 t. salt
3/4 c. milk

1 egg, beaten
1/3 c. oil
1 c. blueberries
1 t. lemon zest
1/4 to 1/2 c. butter, melted

Sift together flour, 1/4 cup sugar, baking powder and salt into a
medium mixing bowl; make a well in the center of flour mixture.
Combine milk, egg and oil, add to dry ingredients. Stir quickly, just
until dry ingredients are moistened. Toss together blueberries and
2 tablespoons sugar; gently stir into batter along with lemon zest. Fill
greased muffin tins 2/3 full. Bake at 400 degrees for 25 minutes.
While muffins are still warm, brush with melted butter then sprinkle
tops with remaining sugar. Makes one dozen.

Mini muffins are just right
for between-meal snacks.
Bake the batter in mini
muffin tins, then store
them in your cookie jar
for a quick treat!

Walnut & Pumpkin Bread

Christine Sullivan
San Ramon, CA

This makes a wonderful after school treat served with icy milk.

2 c. all-purpose flour
1/2 t. baking soda
1 t. cinnamon
1/2 t. allspice
1 c. sugar
1/2 t. salt
1/2 t. nutmeg

2 t. baking powder
1 c. pumpkin
1/2 c. milk
2 eggs, beaten
1/2 c. butter, softened
1 c. walnuts, chopped

Sift all dry ingredients together; add pumpkin and milk. Add eggs, one at a time, beating in. Stir in butter and walnuts. Pour into 2 well greased 9"x5" loaf pans. Bake in a 350 degree oven for 45 to 50 minutes or until bread tests done.

Spice Muffins

Annette Wesgaites
Hazelton, PA

My favorite recipe simply because they're so easy to make!

2 c. biscuit baking mix
1/2 c. milk
2 T. sugar
1/4 c. applesauce

2 T. brown sugar, packed
1/2 t. cinnamon
1/2 t. nutmeg

Place all ingredients into a medium bowl. Stir together for one minute with wooden spoon. Fill greased muffin tins 2/3 full. Bake at 350 degrees for 15 minutes. Makes one dozen muffins.

The only thing to do
is to hug one's friends tight
and do one's job.

-Edith Wharton

Apple-Oatmeal Coffee Cake

Winnette Anker
South Holland, IL

*A tasty coffee cake any time of year, but especially good
with just-picked apples from the orchard.*

1 c. all-purpose flour
3/4 t. baking soda
1/2 t. salt
1/4 t. allspice
1/4 t. cinnamon
1 c. sugar
1 c. quick-cooking oats

1/2 c. oil
1 egg
1 t. vanilla extract
1 c. apple, peeled, cored and
    chopped
1/3 c. nuts, chopped

Mix dry ingredients together in bowl. Add remaining ingredients;
mixture will be quite thick. Pour into a greased 8"x8" pan. Bake at
350 degrees for 35 minutes. Makes 9 servings.

*If you've been apple picking,
share your bounty with a friend.
Line a basket with a red checked
cloth, still warm apple-oatmeal
coffee cake and lots of crunchy
apples...don't forget the recipe!*

Orange-Nut Bread

The Governor's Inn
Ludlow, VT

We like to serve this for a leisurely breakfast or brunch.

2 c. all-purpose flour
1/2 t. salt
1 t. baking powder
1/4 t. baking soda
2/3 c. sugar
1/3 c. unsalted butter, softened
2 eggs

1/2 c. orange juice with pulp
1/2 c. water
1/2 t. vanilla extract
1/2 t. orange extract
1 c. walnuts, chopped

Grease three 6"x3-1/2" loaf pans; set aside. In a medium bowl, sift together flour, salt, baking powder and baking soda. In a large bowl, cream together the sugar and butter. Beat in the eggs, one at a time. Stir in the orange juice and water alternately with the flour mixture. Add the extracts and walnuts and pour into the prepared loaf pans. Bake in a 350 degree oven for 40 to 45 minutes. Remove from the pan, cool and wrap. Chill well before serving. Makes 3 small loaves.

Orange-Cream Cheese Spread:

3 8-oz. pkgs. cream cheese, softened
3 to 4 T. powdered sugar

1 navel orange, unpeeled and chopped

In a food processor with steel blade in place, combine the cream cheese, powdered sugar and orange. Process to a thick spread. Refrigerate for several hours to blend flavors. Spread lightly on sliced orange-nut bread.

The greatest pleasure I know
is to do a good action by stealth
and have it found out by accident.

-Charles Lamb

Maple Cornbread

Roxanne Bixby
West Franklin, NH

*This tasty cornbread can be served with sausage and
eggs for breakfast or with a homestyle dinner.*

1 c. plus 2 T. cornmeal
1 c. plus 2 T. whole wheat flour
1 T. baking powder
1/2 t. salt

1 egg, beaten
1/2 c. maple syrup
3/4 c. milk
3 T. shortening, melted

In a large bowl, mix cornmeal, flour, baking powder and salt. Add egg, maple syrup, milk and shortening. Stir until well blended; do not beat. Pour into a well greased 9"x9" pan or 12 greased muffin cups. Bake at 400 degrees for 20 minutes.

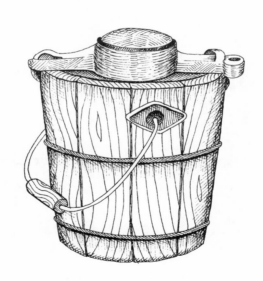

*The kids will love eating "ears" of cornbread... just spoon
the batter into vintage corn-shaped pans!*

Morning Glory Muffins

Cindy McAllister
Sheridan, MI

I like these because they freeze well. Just make several batches,
freeze and then easily reheat whenever you want them.

2 c. all-purpose flour
1-1/4 c. sugar
2 t. baking soda
2 t. cinnamon
1/2 t. salt
2 c. carrots, grated
1/2 c. flaked coconut

1/2 c. raisins
1 apple, peeled, cored and diced
1/2 c. walnuts, chopped
3 eggs
1 c. oil
2 t. vanilla extract

In a large bowl, combine flour, sugar, baking soda, cinnamon and salt.
Stir in carrots, coconut, raisins, apple and nuts. In a separate bowl,
beat together eggs, oil and vanilla. Stir egg mixture into flour mixture.
Spoon into greased muffin cups, filling to the top. Bake at 350 degrees
for 20 minutes. Makes 14 large muffins.

Host a casual outdoor breakfast
for friends and family.
Toss quilts over tables and serve
baskets of warm muffins,
fresh fruit, quick breads and
homemade jams. Pint-size
bottles of juice and milk can be
kept cold in an ice-filled
galvanized bucket.

Cherry Coffee Cake

*Gloria Kaufmann
Orrville, OH*

*The yeast gives this coffee cake a light texture and we
think the cherry pie filling makes it special!*

4½ tsp.

2 pkgs. active dry yeast
2/3 c. warm water
18-1/4 oz. box yellow cake
  mix, divided
2 eggs
1 c. all-purpose flour

14-1/2 oz. can cherry pie filling
2 T. sugar
5 T. margarine, melted
1 c. powdered sugar
1 T. water
1 T. corn syrup

Blend yeast into water until yeast is dissolved. In a separate bowl, mix
1-1/2 cups of cake mix with yeast, eggs and flour. Beat for 2 minutes.
Spread in a greased 13"x9" pan. Top with pie filling and sprinkle with
sugar. Mix remaining cake mix with margarine until crumbly; sprinkle
over pie filling. Bake at 375 degrees for 30 minutes. Mix together
powdered sugar, water and corn syrup; drizzle over warm cake.

Kindness is never wasted.

-S.H. Simmons

Buttermilk-Spice Bread

Joanna Rouse
Bethlehem, PA

I always bake two loaves of this bread because it disappears so fast!

1/4 c. butter
1 c. sugar
1 egg
1 c. buttermilk
1 t. baking soda

2 c. all-purpose flour
1/4 t. salt
1/3 c. sugar
1 T. cinnamon

Cream butter, sugar and egg. Add buttermilk, baking soda, flour and salt; mix well. Combine sugar and cinnamon; set aside. In greased 9"x5" loaf pan, place, in order, 1/3 of batter, 1/2 of cinnamon mix, 1/3 of batter, remaining cinnamon mix then remaining batter. Bake at 375 degrees for 50 minutes or until knife inserted in the center comes out clean.

Take time to laugh, it's the music of the soul.

-Anonymous

Pumpkin-Chocolate Chip Muffins

Kim Martin
Edmond, OK

A favorite recipe shared with me by my friend,
Jane...we both just love these muffins!

4 eggs
1 c. sugar
1/2 c. brown sugar, packed
15-oz. can pumpkin
1-1/2 c. oil

2 c. all-purpose flour
2 t. baking soda
2 t. baking powder
1 t. cinnamon
1 to 2 c. chocolate chips

In a large bowl, mix together eggs, sugar, brown sugar, pumpkin and oil. In a separate bowl, combine flour, baking soda, baking powder and cinnamon. Blend flour mixture into the egg mixture; add chocolate chips. Fill greased muffin cups 2/3 full. Bake at 400 degrees for 15 to 20 minutes. Makes 2 dozen muffins.

During your next autumn bonfire enjoy a warm and tasty apple treat! Slide an apple on a metal skewer and roast until warmed throughout. Slice and enjoy with caramel sauce or sprinkled with cinnamon and sugar.

Spicy Buttermilk Coffee Cake

Sue Collins
Valencia, CA

Fills the house with a wonderful aroma while it's baking; it's sure to please everyone!

2-1/2 c. all-purpose flour
1/2 t. salt
2 t. cinnamon, divided
1/4 t. ginger
1 c. brown sugar, packed
3/4 c. sugar

3/4 c. oil
1 c. walnuts, chopped
1 t. baking soda
1 t. baking powder
1 egg, beaten
1 c. buttermilk

Mix flour, salt, one teaspoon cinnamon, ginger, brown sugar, sugar and oil together in a bowl. Remove 3/4 cup of this mixture and add it to walnuts with remaining one teaspoon cinnamon. Mix well and set aside. To the remaining batter, add baking soda, baking powder, egg and buttermilk; mix. Pour batter into well-greased 13"x9" pan and sprinkle the walnut mixture evenly over the surface. Bake at 350 degrees for 35 to 40 minutes. Makes 12 servings.

Gather together your best-loved family recipes and share them on handmade photo recipe cards. Glue a color copy of Aunt Allie in the corner of an index card then write out her famous recipe for Kentucky pie.

Cinnamon Twist Bread

Emily Nelsen
Jerome, ID

This is for those mornings when cold cereal just won't work!

2 c. all-purpose flour
1 c. plus 2 T. sugar, divided
4 t. baking powder
2-1/2 t. cinnamon, divided
1-1/4 t. salt

1 c. buttermilk
1/3 c. oil
2 t. vanilla extract
2 eggs
2 t. butter, softened

Grease and flour bottom only of 9"x5" loaf pan. In large bowl, combine flour, one cup sugar, baking powder, 1-1/2 teaspoons cinnamon, salt, buttermilk, oil, vanilla and eggs. Beat 3 minutes at medium speed; pour batter into pan. In a small bowl, combine butter, remaining sugar and remaining cinnamon. Sprinkle over batter and swirl lightly to marble. Bake at 350 degrees for 45 to 50 minutes or until toothpick comes out clean. Remove from pan before slicing.

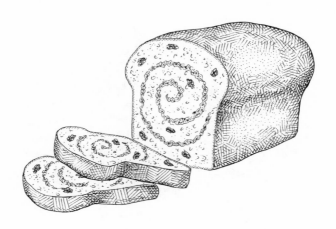

Pressed-glass jars can store everything from flour and
sugar to cookie cutters and tins of sprinkles!
Easily found at tag sales or flea markets,
they'll bring back fond memories of Mom's kitchen.

Nutmeg Streusel Muffins

Gail Prather
Bethel, MN

You'll enjoy these yummy muffins topped with brown sugar!

2 c. all-purpose flour, divided
1 c. brown sugar, packed
1/2 c. butter, softened
1-1/2 t. baking powder
1-1/2 t. nutmeg

1/2 t. baking soda
1/2 t. salt
2/3 c. buttermilk
1 egg

In a large bowl, combine 1-1/3 cups flour and brown sugar. Cut in butter until crumbly and reserve 1/2 cup for streusel topping. In the same bowl, add remaining ingredients; stir until just moistened. Spoon into greased muffin pans and sprinkle with reserved streusel mixture. Bake at 400 degrees for 18 to 22 minutes or until lightly browned. Let stand 3 minutes; remove from pan. Makes 18 muffins.

Celebrate September 28, Good Neighbor Day, by taking a big basket of freshly-baked goodies next door!

Sugar-Topped Coffee Cake

Tina Wright
Atlanta, GA

A chocolate lover's dream!

2 c. all-purpose flour
1 t. baking powder
1/2 t. baking soda
1/2 t. salt
1-1/4 c. sugar, divided
5 T. butter, softened
2 eggs

1 t. vanilla extract
1 c. sour cream
3/4 c. walnuts, coarsely chopped
1/3 c. mini-chocolate chips
1-1/2 T. cocoa
3/4 t. cinnamon
Garnish: powdered sugar

Blend together flour, baking powder, baking soda and salt. In a separate bowl, cream together one cup sugar and butter. Beat in eggs, one at a time; stir in vanilla. Alternate egg mixture and sour cream with dry ingredients; set aside. Mix walnuts, chocolate chips, remaining sugar, cocoa powder and cinnamon. Spoon half of batter into a greased and floured tube or Bundt® pan. Sprinkle half of the nut mixture evenly over batter, top with remaining batter and sprinkle walnut mixture on top. Use a butter knife to swirl batter to make a marbled coffee cake. Bake at 350 degrees for about 40 to 50 minutes. Cool completely and dust with powdered sugar.

Fill a large basket with bright oranges and clementines for a beautiful breakfast centerpiece!

Apple Upside-Down Muffins

Becky Sykes
Gooseberry Patch

Our three girls love these and they're so easy to make.

1-1/2 c. all-purpose flour
2 t. baking powder
1/2 c. sugar
1/2 t. salt
1/2 t. cinnamon
1/4 t. nutmeg
1/4 c. plus 3 T. butter, divided

1/2 c. buttermilk
1 egg, beaten
1 c. apple, peeled, cored and
  grated
1/3 c. brown sugar, packed
1/2 c. pecans, chopped

Combine flour, baking powder, sugar, salt, cinnamon and nutmeg.
With pastry cutter, cut in 1/4 cup butter. Combine buttermilk and egg
and add to flour mixture, along with apple; stir to moisten. Over low
heat, melt remaining butter in a small saucepan and stir in brown
sugar. Spoon one teaspoon brown sugar mixture into each cup of a
greased 12-count muffin tin. Add pecans to each muffin cup. Spoon
batter into cups and bake at 375 degrees for about 20 minutes.
Remove from pan and serve with nut side up. Makes 12 muffins.

*Get all the moms in the
neighborhood together for
a morning muffin swap!
Ask everyone to bring a dozen
muffins to share and some
extras to sample!
You'll have a fun time
chatting and catching up on
neighborhood happenings!*

Raspberry Coffee Cake

Susan Brzozowski
Ellicott City, MD

Your home will smell wonderful while this is baking.

2-1/4 c. all-purpose flour
1 c. sugar, divided
3/4 c. margarine
1/2 t. baking powder
1/2 t. baking soda
1/4 t. salt
3/4 c. sour cream

1 t. almond extract
2 eggs, divided
8-oz. pkg. cream cheese,
   softened
1/2 c. raspberry preserves
1/2 c. almonds, sliced

Grease and flour bottom and sides of 9" or 10" springform pan. In large bowl, combine flour and 3/4 cup sugar. Using pastry blender or fork, cut in margarine until mixture resemble coarse crumbs. Reserve one cup of crumb mixture. To remaining crumb mixture, add baking powder, baking soda, salt, sour cream, almond extract and one egg; blend well. Spread batter over bottom and 2 inches up sides of greased and floured pan. Batter should be about 1/4 inch thick on sides. In small bowl, combine cream cheese, remaining sugar and one egg; blend well. Pour into batter-lined pan. Carefully spoon preserves evenly over cream cheese mixture. In small bowl, combine reserved crumb mixture and sliced almonds. Sprinkle over preserves. Bake at 350 degrees for 45 to 55 minutes or until cream cheese filling is set and crust is deep golden brown. Cool for 15 minutes. Then remove sides of pan. Makes 16 servings.

*...all that's dear comes
from a friend.*

-Horace

Coffee Can Molasses Bread

Megan Brooks
Antioch, TN

Grandma's recipe for the best quick bread ever!

2 c. whole-wheat flour
1/2 c. cornmeal
2 t. baking soda
1/2 t. salt
2 c. buttermilk

1/2 c. molasses
1/2 c. raisins
1/2 c. dried apples, finely
  chopped

Combine all ingredients together in a large bowl. Grease and flour 2, one-pound coffee cans, divide batter equally and spoon inside; let stand for 30 minutes. Bake at 350 degrees for 50 to 55 minutes or until the top is golden and a knife inserted in center comes out clean. Remove cans from oven and let cool 15 minutes. Remove loaves from cans and cool completely. Makes 2 loaves.

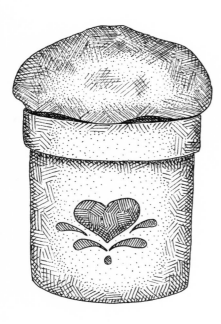

A square of unglazed terra cotta tile makes a perfect bread warmer. Warm the tile in a 350 degree oven for 15 minutes, then carefully slip it between 2 potholders you've stitched together on only 3 sides.

Huckleberry-Lemon Muffins

Debbie Stephens
Colbert, WA

*If you can't find huckleberries, you can substitute blueberries
for these muffins; they'll be just as tasty!*

1-3/4 c. all-purpose flour
1/3 c. sugar
2-1/2 t. baking powder
3/4 t. salt
1 egg, beaten

1 c. lemon yogurt
1/3 c. oil
2 T. milk
1/2 to 1 t. lemon zest
3/4 c. huckleberries

In a large bowl, combine flour, sugar, baking powder and salt. In a
medium bowl, combine egg, yogurt, oil, milk and lemon zest; stir well.
Add egg mixture all at once to flour mixture. Stir just until dry ingredients are moistened, batter should be lumpy. Gently fold berries into
batter. Fill greased muffin cups 2/3 full. Bake at 400 degrees 20 to
25 minutes or until golden and toothpick inserted into center comes
out clean. Serve warm. Makes one dozen.

*If you're saying "goodbye" to
a friend, send along some
home-baked treats,
then fill a box with favorite
photos, notecards, stamps and
an address book; wrap it all
up in a road map.*

Fruit Coffee Cake

Georgia Zerbe
South Bend, IN

*My Aunt Jean gave me this recipe when I was about 13 years old.
I like it because it's easy to make and most of the ingredients
are already in my kitchen pantry.*

2 sticks butter
1 c. sugar
3 eggs
2 T. milk
1 t. vanilla extract

2 c. all-purpose flour
2 t. baking soda
1/8 t. salt
21-oz. can fruit pie filling
Garnish: powdered sugar

Cream together butter and sugar. Blend in eggs, milk and vanilla. Sift together flour, baking soda and salt, combine with egg mixture. Spread 3/4 of batter in a greased and floured 13"x9" pan. Spread fruit filling over batter, add remaining batter on top. Sprinkle entire top with powdered sugar and bake at 350 degrees for 45 minutes.

*Do you have an album full
of old photos from school? Pull out
all the funniest ones...slumber
parties, proms or band camp, make
color copies and slip them into
invitations for all your girlfriends.
Enjoy coffee and dessert
together...and a lot
of laughs, too!*

Quick Breads, Muffins & Coffee Cakes

Cherry-Chip Bread

Vicki Grounds
Woodland Park, CO

Great flavors; almost like a chocolate covered cherry!

2 c. all-purpose flour
1 c. sugar
1-1/2 t. baking powder
1/2 t. baking soda
1/2 t. salt
1/4 c. margarine

3/4 c. water
1 egg, beaten
3/4 c. maraschino cherries,
    drained and chopped
1/2 c. mini-chocolate chips

Combine flour, sugar, baking powder, baking soda and salt. Cut in margarine until particles are the size of coarse meal. Stir in water and egg, fold in cherries and chips and pour batter into a lightly oiled 9"x5" pan. Bake at 350 degrees for 50 to 60 minutes. Cool in pan for 10 minutes, remove from pan and cool completely on wire rack.

When friendship once is rooted fast,
it is a plant no storm can blast.

-19th century calling card verse

55

Oatmeal Muffins

Barbara Nicol
Marysville, OH

*A recipe from my Fairbanks High School home
economics class...they're still my favorite.*

1 T. lemon juice	1/2 c. shortening, melted
1 c. milk	1 c. all-purpose flour
1 c. quick-cooking oats	1 t. baking powder
1 egg	1/2 t. salt
1/2 c. brown sugar, packed	1/2 t. baking soda

Add lemon juice to milk and let stand at room temperature for 10 to
15 minutes before using. Soak oats in milk mixture for one hour; add
egg and beat well. Blend in brown sugar and add cooled shortening.
Sift flour with baking powder, salt and baking soda. Combine with oat
mixture and stir by hand for 20 strokes. Fill greased muffin pans
2/3 full; bake in a preheated 400 degree oven for 15 to 20 minutes.
Makes 12 muffins.

*An old-fashioned oatmeal
box would be the perfect
container for these oatmeal
muffins. Line it with wax
paper and add the
muffins. Tie closed with
a homespun bow.*

Blueberry Cream Coffee Cake

Stephanie Moon
Boise, ID

A traditional recipe, but still a favorite of mine!

2/3 c. plus 2 T. sugar, divided
1/4 c. butter, softened
1 egg
1/4 t. lemon extract
1 c. plus 3 T. all-purpose flour,
    divided
1/2 T. baking powder

1/2 t. salt
1/2 t. cinnamon, divided
1/2 c. milk
1 c. blueberries
4 oz. cream cheese, cubed
1 T. cold butter

Cream 2/3 cup sugar and butter until light and fluffy. Blend in egg and lemon extract. In a separate bowl, combine one cup flour, baking powder, salt and 1/4 teaspoon cinnamon. Add alternately with milk and creamed mixture. Toss blueberries with one tablespoon flour, fold in batter with cream cheese and pour into greased and floured 9" round pan. To prepare topping, combine remaining sugar, flour and cinnamon. Cut in butter until mixture resembles coarse crumbs. ·Sprinkle evenly over batter. Bake at 375 degrees for 30 minutes or until cake tests done. Makes 6 servings.

I with you, and you with me,
miles are short with company.

-G. Eliot

57

Sweet Corn-Buttermilk Bread

Christy Doyle
Baton Rouge, LA

*You can bake these in old-fashioned corn muffin pans or
in a cast iron skillet; just cut into wedges and serve.*

1-1/4 c. cornmeal
1 c. all-purpose flour
2/3 c. sugar
1/2 t. salt
2/3 c. brown sugar, packed

1 t. baking soda
1 egg
1 c. buttermilk
3/4 c. oil

In a bowl, stir together corn meal, flour, sugar, salt, brown sugar and soda. In a second bowl, whisk together egg, buttermilk and oil. Add to dry ingredients all at once, stirring until just blended. Spoon into well greased 9" pan. Bake at 425 degrees for 20 minutes or until golden brown.

*Take a day trip with just the girls! Load up the car and head
out... flea markets, tag sales, shopping or a movie, then
stop at a small town diner for a home-cooked meal!*

Gingersnap Mini Muffins

Gail Prather
Bethel, MN

*You'll love these sweet and spicy, tiny muffins! They're great
for school lunch boxes or a take-along snack.*

1/4 c. sugar
1/4 c. brown sugar, packed
2/3 c. molasses
1 egg
1-1/2 t. baking soda
1 t. cinnamon

1 t. ginger
1/2 t. ground cloves
2 t. lemon zest
2-1/2 c. all-purpose flour
1 c. sour cream
Garnish: powdered sugar

In a large mixer bowl, combine sugar, brown sugar, molasses, egg,
baking soda, cinnamon, ginger, cloves and zest. Beat at medium speed
until well mixed. Add flour and sour cream; continue beating well.
Spoon batter into greased mini muffin pans, filling cups 3/4 full. Bake
at 375 degrees for 11 to 14 minutes or until toothpick inserted in
center comes out clean. Let stand 5 minutes, remove from pan.
Sprinkle with powdered sugar. Makes 2-1/2 dozen.

*Let someone know you think
they're the best! Tie a blue
ribbon around a loaf of bread
or a basket of muffins.
Add a tag that says
"Blue Ribbon Friend!"*

Applechip Coffee Cake

*Glenda Hill
Columbus, OH*

*Use different types of apples to change the taste...spicy Fuji,
crunchy Red Delicious or tart Granny Smith.*

1-1/2 c. plus 2 T. all-purpose
   flour, divided
3/4 c. sugar, divided
2 t. baking powder
1 t. salt
1 egg, beaten

1/2 c. milk
1/4 c. oil
1 c. apple, peeled, cored and
   finely chopped
2 t. cinnamon
2 T. butter

In a large bowl, mix 1-1/2 cups flour, 1/2 cup sugar, baking powder
and salt. In a separate bowl, blend together egg, milk, oil and apple.
Slowly add to the dry ingredients. Spread batter into a greased
9"x9" pan. Blend together remaining flour, sugar, cinnamon and
butter. Sprinkle topping over cake. Bake at 400 degrees for 25 to
30 minutes.

Friends are a second existence.

-Baltasar Gracian

Irish Soda Bread

Claire McGeough
Lebanon, NJ

Since my sister Joan gave me this recipe, it's become my favorite!

4 c. all-purpose flour
1/4 c. sugar
1 t. baking powder
2 T. caraway seeds
1/4 c. butter

2 c. raisins
1-1/3 c. buttermilk
1 egg
1 t. baking soda
1 egg yolk, beaten

Mix flour, sugar and baking powder into mixing bowl; stir in caraway seeds. Cut in butter until mixture looks like coarse meal. Stir in raisins and set aside. Combine buttermilk, egg and baking soda; stir into flour mixture just enough to moisten dry ingredients. Turn onto floured board and knead lightly until dough is smooth. Shape in a ball and place into a greased 2-quart casserole dish. Brush with egg yolk and bake at 375 degrees for one hour. Cool bread for 10 minutes before removing from casserole dish.

Settle into a cozy corner and
take time to do some of those
things you've been meaning
to... call old friends,
write a long letter,
learn to cross-stitch,
sort through Mom's recipe box
or re-read a favorite book.

Peanut Butter Bread

Michele Cutler
Sandy, UT

A yummy bread we love to enjoy fresh out
of the oven on cold, wintry days.

3/4 c. sugar
1/2 c. peanut butter
1 t. vanilla extract
1-3/4 c. milk

2-1/4 c. all-purpose flour
4 t. baking powder
1/2 t. salt

In a large bowl, blend together sugar, peanut butter and vanilla. Gradually pour in milk; mix well. Sift together flour, baking powder and salt; add to peanut butter mixture. Spread batter into a greased 9"x5" loaf pan. Bake at 350 degrees for 45 to 50 minutes.

Before your next family reunion, ask everyone to bring their favorite recipes, as well as any stories about the recipe. Perhaps it's been handed down for generations or maybe a tasty dish was created by accident. Retype the recipes and stories then make plenty of copies to share at the next reunion!

Coconut Cream Muffins

Stephanie Moon
Boise, ID

*I have many recipes tucked away, but this
favorite is one I wanted to share.*

1-1/4 c. all-purpose flour
1 t. baking powder
1/4 t. salt
1-1/2 t. vanilla extract
1/4 t. almond extract

2/3 c. half-and-half
1/2 c. butter, softened
3/4 c. sugar
2 eggs
1-3/4 c. flaked coconut

Blend together flour, baking powder and salt in a small bowl. Stir extracts into half-and-half. Beat butter in large bowl with an electric mixer on high speed for one minute. Gradually add sugar and beat until fluffy. Reduce mixer speed to medium and beat in eggs until blended. Reduce mixer speed to low. Alternately beat in flour and cream mixtures, beginning and ending with the flour, just until blended. Stir in coconut. Fill greased and floured muffin tins 2/3 full and bake at 350 degrees for 18 to 20 minutes or until muffins test done. Cool in pan on wire rack. Makes one dozen muffins.

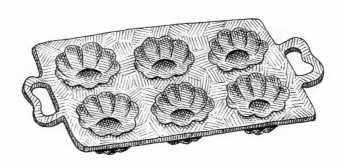

The hand that gives gathers.

-Old English Proverb

Fresh Strawberry Muffins

June Cavarretta
West Dundee, IL

I think this is the best strawberry muffin recipe!

3 c. all-purpose flour
2 c. sugar
1 t. baking powder
1 t. salt
1 t. cinnamon

4 eggs, beaten
1-1/4 c. oil
2-1/2 c. fresh strawberries,
          sliced and slightly mashed

Combine dry ingredients in large mixing bowl. In small bowl, combine eggs and oil. Stir strawberries into egg mixture. Blend in flour mixture until thoroughly combined; do not over beat. Spoon into greased muffin tins. Bake at 400 degrees for 25 minutes. Makes approximately 2 dozen.

Live your life while you have it. Life is a splendid gift;
there is nothing small about it.

-Florence Nightingale

Banana & Walnut Bread

*Corky Hines
Walworth, NY*

A fruit-filled quick bread! It's easily doubled and frozen.

1/4 c. shortening
1/4 c. margarine
1 c. sugar
2 eggs
1 c. bananas, mashed
1-1/2 c. all-purpose flour

1 t. baking soda
1/4 t. salt
1/4 t. cinnamon
1/2 c. quick oats
1/2 c. blueberries
1/2 c. nuts, chopped

In large bowl, cream shortening, margarine and sugar together. Add eggs, one at a time, mixing well after each addition; stir in bananas. In a separate bowl, sift together flour, baking soda, salt and cinnamon. Stir oats, blueberries and nuts into dry ingredients. Carefully blend the dry mixture into the creamed mixture, stirring only to moisten. Pour batter into a well greased 9"x5" loaf pan. Bake at 350 degrees for 50 to 55 minutes, or until toothpick inserted into center comes out clean. Cool for 10 minutes before removing from pan. Allow bread to cool completely on a wire rack.

If you're hosting a breakfast or brunch, pamper coffee-lovers with fresh cream and shakers of nutmeg, cinnamon and cocoa. Tea drinkers will enjoy slices of lemon, flavored honey and a variety of teas to choose from.

Betsy Bread

Kelly Elliott
Fairview, TN

My favorite bread to serve with soup or stew.

2 c. cornmeal
1 c. all-purpose flour
1 c. sugar
2 c. buttermilk

3 T. oil
1 t. salt
1 t. baking soda

Mix all ingredients together. Pour into a greased 9"x5" loaf pan. Bake at 350 degrees for one hour. Makes one loaf.

Give someone an unexpected gift... the school bus driver, the mailman, a new neighbor, or drop off some toys or treats at the cat or dog shelter... just because. It will make your day and someone else's, too!

Yeast Breads

Mixed Berry JAM

Peppi Bread

Donna Dugas
Ulm, MT

A wonderful bread for gift-giving. Tuck it back in the coffee can after it's cooled, then tie a homespun bow around the can.

1 pkg. active dry yeast	2 T. oil
1/2 c. warm water	12-oz. can evaporated milk
1/4 t. ginger	2 c. all-purpose flour
2 T. sugar	2 c. whole-wheat flour
1/2 t. salt	

Mix yeast in warm water until yeast dissolves. Add ginger, sugar, salt, oil and milk. Add flours, one cup at a time; stir well after each. Knead 5 or 6 times. Divide dough between 2, well greased, one-pound coffee cans. Cover with cloth and let rise in warm place until dough is one inch above the top of the cans; about one hour. Bake at 350 degrees for 40 minutes. Remove immediately from cans. Makes 2, one-pound loaves of bread.

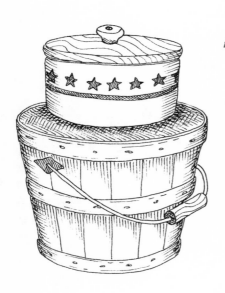

Host a chili cook-off! Ask neighbors to bring a pot of their "secret recipe" chili to share, then have a friendly judging for the best. . . mild, five-alarm and vegetarian. You provide lots of bread and butter, soda and bright red bandannas for great lap-size napkins.

Grandma's Bread

Thais Menges
Three Rivers, MI

*This is my sweet grandma's recipe for a delicious
bread that I make all the time.*

1 pkg. active dry yeast
1/2 c. lukewarm water
1-1/2 t. salt
1/2 c. sugar
2 T. shortening

1 c. boiling water
1 c. cold milk
2 eggs, beaten
6-1/2 to 7 c. all-purpose flour

Dissolve yeast in lukewarm water. Place salt, sugar and shortening
in a large mixing bowl. Pour boiling water over mixture, stirring
constantly to melt shortening. Add milk and eggs; mix well. Add
yeast and stir until well blended. Add 3-1/2 cups flour and mix for
3 minutes. Add enough of the remaining flour to make a moderately
stiff dough. Turn out onto lightly floured surface and knead until
smooth and elastic, about 8 to 10 minutes. Shape into a ball, place
dough in a lightly greased bowl and turn once to grease surface. Cover
and let rise in a warm place until double, about one hour. Turn out
onto lightly floured surface and knead again, about 3 to 4 minutes.
Place dough back into bowl and let rise about 45 minutes. Punch
dough back into bowl and let rise for 45 minutes.
Punch dough down, turn onto lightly floured
surface. Divide dough in half and
place each half into a 9"x5" loaf pan.
Let rise until double in size. Bake
at 350 degrees for 40 to 50 minutes.
Remove bread from pans and cool
on wire racks.

Light tomorrow with today.

-Elizabeth Barrett Browning

Pop-Up Bread

Anne Olson
Sequim, WA

My oldest son and I used to make this bread when I got home from work, now that he's grown he still makes it.

3 to 3-1/2 c. all-purpose flour, divided
1 pkg. instant yeast
1/2 c. milk
1/2 c. water
1/2 c. oil
1/4 c. sugar
1 t. salt
2 eggs, beaten
1 c. sharp Cheddar Cheese, shredded

Stir together 1-1/2 cups flour and yeast. Heat milk, water, oil, sugar and salt until warm; stirring to blend. Add liquid ingredients to flour mixture and beat until smooth, about 300 strokes by hand. Blend in eggs and cheese. Stir in remaining flour and beat until smooth, about 150 strokes. Divide into 2 greased one-pound coffee cans. Cover with plastic lids and let rise about one hour. Remove lids and bake at 375 degrees for 30 top 35 minutes. Cool in cans 15 minutes before removing.

Make your own hamburger buns; they're so easy!
Just roll dough in balls and place in a lightly oiled
Yorkshire pudding pan. Let dough rise then,
bake according to your recipe.

Whole-Wheat Bread

Jane Ramicone
Berea, OH

A family favorite since I started making it in 4-H many years ago.
Try it warm with cinnamon butter, honey or fruit preserves.

4 c. milk
1/4 c. sugar
4 t. salt
1 pkg. active dry yeast

5 c. whole-wheat flour
2 T. shortening
5 c. all-purpose flour

Heat milk slowly in a small pan until tiny bubbles appear around the edges. Remove from heat and add sugar and salt; stir and cool to lukewarm. Add yeast. In a large bowl, combine yeast mixture with whole-wheat flour, beating thoroughly until bubbles are formed. Beat in shortening. Using a heavy-duty mixer, add enough all-purpose flour to form a dough which cleans the sides of the bowl. Turn out into a well floured bowl. Let rest 10 minutes. Knead until smooth, elastic and satiny. Place in greased bowl. Cover and let rise in warm place until double. Punch down. Let rise again until double in bulk. Divide into 4 equal portions. Round each into smooth ball, cover well and let rest 10 to 15 minutes. Mold into loaves. Place into greased 9"x5" bread pans and let rise until double in bulk. Bake in a moderately high oven, about 375 to 400 degrees for 40 to 45 minutes. Makes 4 one-pound loaves.

Bread is like dresses, hats and shoes. . . in other words, essential!

-Emily Post

Onion & Sour Cream Bread

Rhonda Reeder
Ellicott City, MD

*I let the bread machine do the hard work, then I finish baking
my bread in the oven. Nothing beats the taste of
homemade whole-wheat bread!*

3 c. whole-wheat flour
2 T. sugar
1 t. salt
2 t. active dry yeast

1-oz. pkg. dried onion soup mix
1 c. sour cream
1/2 c. water

Using your manufacturer's manual as a guide, place flour, sugar, salt,
yeast, dried soup, sour cream and water in your bread machine. Select
the manual or dough cycle and let the machine mix and knead your
dough. When the cycle has ended, shape the dough and place in an
oiled 9"x5" loaf pan. Let rise until double in size, then bake at
350 degrees for 25 to 30 minutes.

*Use cookie cutters
to cut shapes from bread
slices...sandwiches the
kids will love!
Stars, hearts, flowers,
snowflakes, mittens...all
make lunchtime more fun!*

Dilly Casserole Bread

Margie Schaffner
Altoona, IA

This has been in our family for years...there's nothing better than the smell of freshly-baked bread filling the air.

1 pkg. active dry yeast
1/4 c. warm water
1 c. warm cottage cheese
2 T. sugar
1 T. dried minced onion
2 T. butter, divided

2 t. dill seed
1-1/2 t. salt, divided
1/4 t. baking soda
1 egg
2-1/4 to 2-1/2 c. all-purpose
  flour

Soften yeast in warm water. Combine cottage cheese, sugar, onion, one tablespoon butter, dill seed, one teaspoon salt, baking soda, egg and yeast in mixing bowl. Add flour to make stiff dough. Cover and let rise until double in size, about 40 minutes. Stir dough down, place into a greased 9"x5" bread pan. Let rise for 40 minutes. Bake at 350 degrees for 40 minutes or until golden brown. Brush with remaining butter and sprinkle lightly with remaining salt. Makes one loaf.

DELUXE MIXING BOWL

You can use rubber stamps to decorate napkins! There are lots of great designs...try paw prints, sunflowers or snowmen!

Two-Herb Loaf

Geneva Rogers
Gillette, WY

We just love this bread filled with herbs and cracked black pepper.

1 pkg. active dry yeast
1/2 t. sugar
2 c. warm water, divided
6 to 6-1/2 c. bread flour, divided
1/2 c. grated Parmesan cheese
1/4 c. olive oil

1 t. salt
1 t. dried basil
1/2 t. dried oregano
1/4 t. pepper
2 T. cornmeal

Dissolve yeast and sugar in 1/2 cup warm water and let stand until foamy. Stir in remaining water, 4 cups of flour, cheese, oil, salt, basil, oregano and pepper. Mix until smooth, adding remaining flour, 1/2 cup at a time, until dough is soft and pulls away from the bowl. Place dough on a lightly floured board and knead 5 minutes. Place dough in an oiled bowl, turning to coat. Cover bowl with a cloth and let rise until double in size, about one hour. Oil 2 large cookie sheets and sprinkle with cornmeal; set aside. Divide dough in half and roll each half into a 16-inch long rope. Place loaves on cornmeal, cover and let rise 45 minutes. Bake at 400 degrees for 30 to 45 minutes or until loaves are golden and sound hollow when tapped.

If you have bread and butter, you have good luck.

-Yiddish proverb

Best Friend Bread

Jana Warnell
Kalispell, MT

While visiting my best friend, her mom was baking a fresh loaf of this bread. It was so good, I asked her to teach me how to make it!

1 pkg. active dry yeast	1 t. salt
1-1/4 c. warm water	2 eggs
1/4 c. sugar	4-1/2 c. all-purpose flour
1/4 c. oil	1/4 c. butter, melted

Dissolve yeast in warm water. Mix sugar, oil, salt and eggs together; stir in yeast mixture. Add flour and knead until smooth. Cover and let rise until double in size. Punch down and turn out onto floured surface. Divide dough into 3 equal pieces. Roll each piece with your hands until you have 3 ropes about 12 inches long. Pinch one end of each of the 3 pieces of dough together and braid dough. Pinch the other ends together to seal, then tuck under. Place on a greased 13"x9" pan and let rise until double again. Pour butter over the top and bake at 350 degrees for 30 minutes.

Fill a basket with a loaf of warm bread and a big jar of homemade noodle soup...perfect for someone feeling under the weather.

Pennsylvania Dutch Loaves

Tina Knotts
Gooseberry Patch

Give a tasty gift! Just wrap these old-fashioned loaves in a square of homespun then tuck them in a yellowware bowl.

4-1/2 to 5 c. all-purpose flour, divided
1 pkg. active dry yeast
1-1/4 c. milk
1/2 c. butter
3/4 c. sugar
1 t. salt
1 egg, beaten
3/4 c. raisins
1/2 c. currants
1/3 c. candied citron, finely chopped
1 c. powdered sugar
1/4 t. vanilla extract
1 to 2 T. milk
Garnish: 1/2 c. blanched almonds, finely chopped

In large mixer bowl, combine 2 cups flour and yeast. In saucepan, heat the milk, butter, sugar and salt until just warm and butter is almost melted. Stir butter mixture into flour; add egg. Beat at low speed for one minute, scraping sides of the bowl. Beat 3 minutes at high speed. Add raisins, currants and citron; mix well. By hand, stir in enough of the remaining flour to make a moderately soft dough. Turn out onto a lightly floured surface; knead 5 to 8 minutes until smooth and elastic. Place dough in a lightly greased bowl; turn once to grease surface. Cover and let rise in a warm place about 1-1/2 hours or until double. Punch dough down; turn out onto a lightly floured surface. Divide into 4 portions. Shape into 6-inch loaves. Place on greased baking sheet 3 inches apart. Cover; let rise again for about one hour. Bake in a 375 degree oven for 20 to 30 minutes or until loaves sound hollow when lightly tapped. Set aside to cool. In medium size bowl, sift powdered sugar; add vanilla extract and enough milk until mixture reaches a drizzling consistency. Spoon over loaves and sprinkle with almonds. Makes 4 loaves.

Powdered Sugar

Julekage

Juanita Williams
Jacksonville, OR

A traditional Norwegian sweet bread.

1-1/2 c. raisins
3/4 c. mixed dried candied fruit, diced
1/2 c. brandy
6 to 7 c. all-purpose flour, divided
4 pkgs. active dry yeast
3/4 c. lukewarm water
2/3 c. plus 2 T. sugar, divided
1/2 c. milk

1 c. unsalted butter
1 t. salt
1 t. rose water
2 t. powdered cardamom
zest of one orange and one lemon
1 egg yolk, beaten
1 T. water
Garnish: sugar and blanched almond halves

Combine raisins, candied fruit and brandy; let stand one hour. Drain, reserving fruit and brandy. Toss fruits with enough flour to lightly coat. Sprinkle yeast in lukewarm water, add 2 tablespoons sugar, cover lightly and set in a warm place for about 10 minutes, or until mixture foams. Scald milk with butter, remaining sugar and salt. When butter has melted, remove milk from heat and stir in rose water, 2 teaspoons reserved brandy mixture, cardamom and zest. Cool to lukewarm and combine with yeast mixture. Gradually add 5 cups of flour. Turn onto a floured board and knead for 10 minutes, adding more flour if needed. When dough is smooth, place in a lightly floured bowl. Dust top of dough with flour, cover lightly and let rise for about 45 minutes to one hour, or until double in bulk and no longer springy when you press it down with your fingertips. Shape dough into one large or 2 small loaves. Combine egg yolk and water; brush over tops of bread. Sprinkle with sugar and blanched almonds. Place loaves in 9"x5" loaf pans. Let rise again until double and bake at 350 degrees for one hour, or until golden. Drizzle with your favorite powdered sugar icing, if desired.

We have been friends together in sunshine and in shade.

-Caroline Norton

Susie's Bread

Regina Ferrigno
Gooseberry Patch

Not only pretty, but great tasting, too!

1-1/4 c. milk, divided
1 pkg. active dry yeast
1/4 c. sugar
1 t. salt
1/4 t. anise seed

2 eggs, beaten
1/4 c. butter, softened
4-1/2 c. all-purpose flour
3 c. powdered sugar

Warm 1/4 cup milk in saucepan; add yeast and set aside. Place 3/4 cup milk in bowl and add sugar, salt and anise seed; stir with a wooden spoon. Add beaten eggs to milk mixture. Stir in butter and mix. Alternate flour and yeast mixture gradually. Dough should be slightly sticky. Flour a bread board and knead dough, adding flour until dough is no longer sticky. Cover dough with a towel and let rise for 2 hours. Knead dough again and place dough on greased cookie sheet. Let dough rise again for 2 hours. Bake at 350 degrees for 35 minutes on the middle rack of the oven. Remove from oven and cool on a rack. Heat 1/4 cup of milk and add powdered sugar until mixture becomes thick, but pourable. Drizzle glaze over bread.

If you're giving a jar of honey butter with your bread, top it off with a fun family photo. Glue a color photocopy of a favorite picture on the lid of your canning jar, then glue the lid inside the screw ring; attach to your jar.

Vermont Graham Bread

Denise Jones
Barre, VT

A great old-fashioned bread my Grandmother always made.

3 c. milk, scalded
1 stick unsalted butter
1 T. salt
1/2 c. molasses

2 pkgs. active dry yeast
1/3 c. lukewarm water
5 c. graham flour
4 c. all-purpose flour

Allow milk to cool slightly, then stir in butter, salt and molasses. When mixture has cooled to warm, sprinkle yeast in water; stir to dissolve. Pour this into the milk mixture, add graham flour until well combined. Cover and let rise 45 minutes to one hour. Stir dough down and add the all-purpose flour; dough will be soft. Let rise again until double in bulk. Divide dough in half and place each half in an oiled 9"x5" loaf pan. Cover and let rise until double in size. Bake at 375 degrees for 35 to 40 minutes.

Bread is the warmest, kindest of words. Write it always with a capital letter, like your own name.

-Russian café sign

English Muffin Loaf

Valerie Busch
Cygnet, OH

I've been making this bread for 17 years and it's always been a family favorite. We love it sliced and sprinkled with sugar and cinnamon or covered with strawberry jam. It's a wonderful gift for neighbors and friends. We've found that even as our children leave the nest, it's a recipe they still ask me to make.

6 c. all-purpose flour, divided
2 pkgs. instant yeast
1 T. sugar
2 t. salt
1/4 t. baking soda
2 c. milk
1/2 c. water
2 T. cornmeal, divided

Sift together 3 cups of flour with other dry ingredients. Heat milk and water to 120 to 130 degrees; add to dry mixture; beat well. Stir in remaining flour to make a stiff batter. Add a tablespoon of cornmeal into the bottom of two 8-1/2"x4-1/2" pans, spoon in batter over cornmeal. Cover, let rise in warm place for 45 minutes. Bake at 400 degrees for 25 minutes. Remove from pans and cool on wire racks.

Old-Fashioned Honey Bread

Rene Ray
Delaware, OH

*A hearty bread that's easy to make. Great sliced for
sandwiches or with a bowl of homemade soup.*

1-1/2 c. water
8 oz. small curd cottage cheese
1/2 c. honey
1/4 c. plus 2 T. butter, divided
1 c. whole-wheat flour

2 T. sugar
2 pkgs. active dry yeast
5-1/2 to 6 c. all-purpose flour
3 t. salt
1 egg

Heat water, cottage cheese, honey and 1/4 cup butter in medium
saucepan until very warm. Combine warm liquid, whole-wheat flour,
sugar, yeast, 2 cups all-purpose flour, salt and egg in a large bowl;
beat 2 minutes at medium speed. By hand, stir in enough remaining
flour to make a stiff dough. Knead dough on a well floured surface
until smooth and elastic, about 2 minutes. Place in greased bowl, turn
to coat. Cover, let rise in warm place until double in size, 45 to
60 minutes. Punch down dough; divide and shape into 2 loaves.
Place in greased 9"x5" pans. Cover and let rise again until light and
double in size, 45 to 60 minutes. Bake at 350 degrees for 40 to
50 minutes or until deep golden brown and loaves sound hollow
when tapped. Immediately remove from pans. Brush warm loaves
with remaining butter.

*Make some honey butter:
1/4 cup honey, 1 cup butter and
1/4 cup powdered sugar.
Blend and spoon into an old-
fashioned crock or canning
jar. A sweet way to say
"Thank-you" to a friend.*

Cinnamon Pull-Apart Bread

Nancy Stinson
Muncie, IN

Years ago I began making this bread for my family every Christmas morning. Although my kids are now grown, they still ask for it when they come home. It's a special treat!

1 pkg. active dry yeast
1/4 c. lukewarm water
1/3 c. plus 3/4 c. sugar, divided
1/3 c. butter
1/2 t. salt
1 c. milk, scalded

3 eggs, beaten
4 c. all-purpose flour
1/2 c. butter, melted
3 t. cinnamon
1/2 c. walnuts, chopped
Garnish: powdered sugar

Dissolve yeast in water. Add 1/3 cup sugar, 1/3 cup butter and salt to milk; cool. Add dissolved yeast, eggs and flour to make a stiff batter. Cover with towel and let rise until double in bulk. Punch down and let rise again until double. Roll dough into small balls about the size of a walnut. Dip balls lightly in melted butter, then roll in mixture of 3/4 cup sugar, cinnamon and nuts. Layer balls loosely in lightly greased tube pan. Cover with towel and let rise for 30 minutes. Bake at 400 degrees for 10 minutes; reduce heat to 350 degrees and bake an additional 30 minutes or until golden. Let cool for 5 minutes and loosen bread from edges of pan. Place plate on top and invert. Sprinkle top lightly with powdered sugar.

No matter where
I serve my guests
It seems they like
My kitchen best

Farmhouse Buttermilk Bread

Cindy Watson
Gooseberry Patch

The best bread for a sandwich...soft and so tasty!

2 pkgs. active dry yeast
1 t. sugar
1 c. warm water
1-1/2 c. buttermilk
3 T. molasses

3 T. oil
1 T. salt
1/2 c. bran
2 c. whole-wheat flour
4 to 4-1/2 c. bread flour

Dissolve yeast and sugar in warm water; set aside 5 to 10 minutes. Blend in buttermilk, molasses, oil and salt. Gradually combine bran and whole-wheat flour into yeast mixture using a heavy duty mixer. Stir in bread flour, 1/2 cup at a time, until a stiff dough forms. Knead dough until smooth, adding more bread flour if dough is sticky. Place dough in an oiled bowl, turning once to coat all sides. Cover and let rise until double in bulk, about one hour. Punch down and knead lightly. Divide dough in half and place each half in an oiled 9"x5" loaf pan. Let rise until almost double, about one hour. Bake at 400 degrees for 45 to 50 minutes.

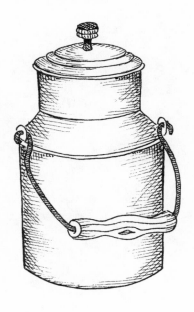

Wrap a loaf of bread in a quick and easy bread cloth. Begin with a 20-inch square of unbleached muslin, then use a permanent pen to write a message or favorite quote around the edges.

Anadama Bread

April Hale
Kirkwood, NY

A hearty brown bread with a crunchy crust, but soft inside.

1/2 c. cornmeal
2 c. boiling water
2 T. shortening
1/2 c. molasses

1 t. salt
1 pkg. cake yeast
1/2 c. warm water
6 c. all-purpose flour

Stir the cornmeal slowly into boiling water; mix well. Add shortening, molasses and salt; set aside to cool. Dissolve the yeast in warm water; about 5 minutes. Add yeast mixture, alternately, with the flour to the lukewarm cornmeal mixture. Knead until smooth and place in large greased bowl. Set in a warm place; cover and let rise until double in bulk. Turn out onto floured board; divide in half. Knead and shape into 2 loaves. Place in greased 9"x5" bread pans and let rise again until double. Bake at 375 degrees for one hour.

The kids can make homemade butter in no time... wonderful on still-warm slices of bread! Just fill a jar with heavy cream, add a tight-fitting lid and roll or shake until the butter forms!

Batter Bread

Theresa Bruner
Delaware, OH

An easy bread to make; no kneading!

2-1/2 c. all-purpose flour
2 T. sugar
1 t. salt
1 pkg. instant yeast

1 c. milk
2 T. shortening
1 egg
1 to 2 t. margarine, melted

Mix flour, sugar, salt and yeast in large bowl. Heat milk and shortening until warm. Beat egg into milk and stir milk mixture into dry ingredients. Scrape batter down from sides of bowl, cover, let rise in warm place until double. Stir batter down to almost original size. Spread in a 9"x5" loaf pan; let rise until double. Bake at 350 degrees for 40 minutes. Remove from pan immediately, brush with margarine and let cool.

Peace and rest at length have come,
all the day's long toil is past; and each heart
is whispering, "Home, Home at last!"

-Thomas Hood

Country Cheddar Loaf

Holly Welsch
Delaware, OH

It gives me such satisfaction to make my own bread and this is a family favorite; we all have difficulty waiting for the bread to cool before we slice it! Our family enjoys it with a hot bowl of chicken noodle soup or a hearty bowl of chili.

4 c. all-purpose flour, divided
2 T. sugar
1 pkg. instant yeast
1 t. salt

1 c. plus 1 T. water, divided
1/3 c. milk
2 c. Cheddar cheese, grated
1 egg white

Combine 1-1/2 cups flour, sugar, yeast and salt. Heat one cup water and milk to 120 to 130 degrees; stir into dry ingredients. Stir in enough remaining flour to make a soft dough. Knead on lightly floured surface until smooth and elastic. Cover; let rest on floured surface for 10 minutes. Knead in cheese. Divide dough into 3 equal pieces; roll each piece to a 14-inch rope. Braid ropes, pinch ends to seal and place on a greased cookie sheet. Cover and let rise for 30 to 45 minutes. Beat egg white with remaining water and brush loaf. Bake at 375 degrees for 30 to 35 minutes. Remove from oven and allow to cool.

Friends are the sunshine of life.

-John Hay

Old World Black Bread

Sharon Stellrecht
Camano Island, WA

When I was an exchange student in Germany, my German "mother" baked delicious Russian-German bread. I couldn't ask her for the recipe due to our language barrier, but years later I found this recipe which is very similar.

3-3/4 c. rye flour
3-3/4 c. all-purpose flour
2 pkgs. active dry yeast
1/2 c. warm water
1/2 c. cocoa
1/4 c. sugar
2 T. caraway seeds

2 t. salt
2 t. instant coffee granules
2 c. water
1/4 c. vinegar
1/4 c. corn syrup
1/4 c. butter

Combine flours in a large bowl; reserve 3 cups of flour mixture. Sprinkle yeast over warm water and stir until dissolved; set aside. In a large bowl, mix together reserved 3 cups of flour, cocoa, sugar, caraway seeds, salt and instant coffee. Combine water, vinegar, corn syrup and butter in a medium-size saucepan. Heat over low heat until just warm, butter does not need to be completely melted. Add to cocoa mixture and blend well. Add dissolved yeast and stir until thoroughly combined. Stir in enough additional flour mixture, one cup at a time, until dough no longer clings to sides of bowl. Turn onto lightly floured board; cover and let rest 10 minutes. Knead dough until smooth and elastic, about 15 minutes. Place in greased bowl and turn greased side up. Cover and let rise in a warm place about one hour or until double. Punch down and turn onto lightly floured board. Divide dough in half; shape each portion into a smooth ball. Place each portion in center of a greased 8" round cake pan. Cover and let rise in warm place about one hour or until double. Bake at 350 degrees for 45 to 50 minutes, or until loaves sound hollow when tapped lightly. Remove from pans and place on wire racks.
Makes 2 loaves.

Wild Rice Bread

Jane Williams
Austin, MN

The wild rice is a tasty surprise baked in the bread!

1 pkg. active dry yeast
1/2 c. plus 1 T. warm water, divided
2 c. milk, scalded and cooled
2 T. butter, melted
2 t. salt
1/2 c. honey
1/2 c. quick-cooking oatmeal
2 c. whole-wheat flour
4-1/2 c. all-purpose flour, divided
1 c. wild rice, cooked
1 egg
1/4 c. sunflower seeds

Dissolve yeast in 1/2 cup water. Add milk, butter, salt and honey. Stir in oatmeal, whole-wheat flour and 2 cups all-purpose flour. Add wild rice, cover and let mixture rest for 15 minutes. Add enough remaining flour until you have a stiff dough. Turn onto a floured surface and knead 10 minutes, adding flour if dough is sticky. Place in a greased bowl, cover and let rise until double. Punch down and shape into 2 loaves and place in greased 9"x5" bread pans; let rise until double. Beat egg with remaining water and brush over loaves, sprinkle with sunflower seeds. Bake at 375 degrees for 45 minutes.

Celebrate National Picnic Month, July, with a family get-together! Sandwiches will look great tucked in colorful galvanized pails. Just wipe down the pails with vinegar and let dry. Apply a spray primer, dry and add any design using acrylic paints. Let the paint dry and spray with satin or matte acrylic sealer.

Focaccia

*Elizabeth Ramicone
Columbus, OH*

Perfect served with pasta!

4 to 4-1/4 c. all-purpose flour,
    divided
1 pkg. fast-rising yeast
1 T. dried basil
1 t. dried thyme

2 garlic cloves, pressed
1/2 t. salt
1-1/2 c. warm water
1 t. honey
2 T. olive oil, divided

Sift together 2 cups of flour, yeast, basil, thyme, garlic and salt.
Combine water and honey; blend into the yeast mixture. Add enough
remaining flour so that dough is smooth and not sticky; knead on a
lightly floured surface for 8 to 10 minutes. Cover and let rise until
double in bulk. Spread one tablespoon of oil on a baking sheet and
transfer dough to the baking sheet; pat into a 14"x10" rectangle.
Brush the dough with the remaining olive oil, let rise 5 minutes and
bake at 375 degrees for 30 minutes or until golden.

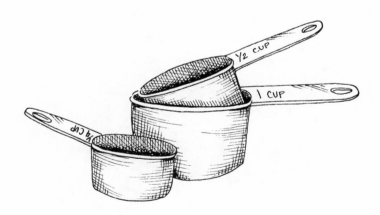

*Try dipping warm slices of focaccia in pesto, marinara
sauce or roasted garlic. . . yummy!*

Mediterranean Loaf

Darrell Lawry
Kissimmee, FL

Try using green olives to give the bread a different flavor.

3 c. bread flour
2 t. instant yeast
2 T. sugar
1 t. salt

1/2 c. black olives, chopped
4 T. olive oil, divided
1-1/4 c. warm water
1/4 c. corn meal

Sift together flour, yeast, sugar and salt. Stir in black olives, 3 tablespoons olive oil and water. Place dough on a lightly floured surface and knead 8 to 10 minutes. Cover and let rise until double, about 45 minutes. Punch down and knead again for 5 minutes. Set aside to rise again until double in bulk. Place a 13"x9" pan of water on the bottom rack of the oven and turn oven to 500 degrees. Evenly spread remaining olive oil on a cookie sheet; sprinkle with cornmeal. Shape dough into a round loaf and place on prepared cookie sheet. Bake at 500 degrees for 15 minutes, reduce heat and bake at 375 degrees for another 20 to 30 minutes or until loaf sounds hollow when tapped.

Cooking is like love. It should be entered into with abandon or not at all.

-Harriet Van Horne

Pesto Marbled Bread

Mary Murray
Gooseberry Patch

*I love the taste of pesto in this bread! It's wonderful
served warm with garlic dipping oil.*

1 pkg. active dry yeast
1 t. sugar
2 c. warm water
2 c. bread flour

1 T. salt
3 T. olive oil
3 c. all-purpose flour
6 T. pesto

Stir yeast and sugar in warm water; set aside 5 minutes. Stir in bread
flour, salt and oil; mix well until smooth. Stir in 2 cups all-purpose
flour and knead on a lightly floured surface; about 10 minutes. Add
enough remaining flour until dough is no longer sticky. Place dough in
an oiled bowl, turning to coat. Cover and let rise in a warm place until
double in size, about 45 minutes. Divide dough in half and roll each
half in an 11"x7" rectangle. Spoon half the pesto in the center of each
rectangle and roll up jelly roll-style, pinch ends to seal. Place seam
side down on an oiled baking sheet; cover and let rise until double.
Bake at 350 degrees for 35 minutes or until loaves sound hollow
when tapped.

*Basket weave bread! You can
easily have a pretty pattern on
loaves of homemade bread!
Just let your dough rise in a
lightly floured basket during its
final rising. Gently remove the
loaf from the basket, place on
an oiled baking sheet
and bake according to
your recipe directions.*

Cheese & Wine Bread

Linda Hurd
Mantua, OH

This recipe makes a large loaf, so it's great for get-togethers.

3 c. all-purpose flour, divided
1 pkg. active dry yeast
1/2 c. dry white wine
1/2 c. butter

2 t. sugar
1 t. salt
3 eggs
1 c. Cheddar cheese, cubed

In a large mixing bowl, combine 1-1/2 cups of the flour and yeast. In saucepan, heat wine, butter, sugar and salt just until warm, stirring constantly until butter almost melts. Add to dry mixture in mixing bowl. Add eggs and beat at low speed for 30 seconds, scraping sides of bowl constantly. Beat 3 minutes at high speed. By hand, stir in the cheese and enough remaining flour to make a soft dough. Turn out onto lightly floured surface; knead until smooth and elastic. Place in lightly greased bowl, turning once to grease surface. Cover and let rise in a warm place until double, about 1-1/2 hours. Punch dough down; cover and let rest 10 minutes. Shape into an 8-inch round loaf. Place in a greased 9" pie plate; cover and let rise in warm place until double, about 40 minutes. Bake in a 375 degree oven for 35 minutes, covering with foil after the first 20 minutes of baking. Makes one large loaf.

The dearest thing in nature is not comparable to the dearest thing of friendship.

-Jeremy Taylor

Cakes & Pies

Very Berry Pie
2 c. blueberries
2 c. strawberries
2 c. raspberries
4 c. baking apples

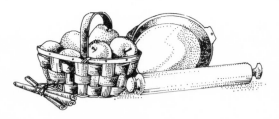

Rustic Country Cherry Pie

Michaela Topalov
Sidney, OH

Long before my best friend, Beth, and I were married with families of our own, we were roommates. I remember Saturday mornings sharing coffee, muffins and dreams of how our lives would change in years to come. Now, Beth's home is always fragrant with something freshly baked and we laughed when she taught me, a hopeless cook, how to make this pie. It may look different, but it always tastes great!

1-1/2 c. all-purpose flour
3/4 stick butter, softened
cold water
1 egg, separated and divided

2 T. cornmeal
1-1/2 lbs. fresh cherries
1/2 c. plus 1-1/2 T. sugar,
  divided

Sift flour, rub in butter with your fingertips and keep lifting until crumbly. Sprinkle in enough cold water to bring together a smooth dough. Knead for one minute, then wrap in wax paper and refrigerate for 30 minutes. Roll pastry out to make a 14-inch circle. Roll pastry around rolling pin and transfer to a lightly greased baking sheet. To keep the pastry from getting soggy, brush the top with egg yolk that has been beaten. Dust the top of the pastry with cornmeal, pile cherries in the center and sprinkle with 1/2 cup of sugar. Turn in edges of pastry over the cherries, brush top with egg white and sprinkle remaining sugar over the top. Bake at 350 degrees on the highest shelf in the oven until the crust is a golden brown, about 35 to 40 minutes.

*Give your cherry pie with
a heart-shaped gift tag
to tell someone they're
your "Sweetie Pie"!*

Harvest Apple Cheesecake

Richard Welsch
Toledo, OH

It's just not autumn until our family takes a trip to the local apple orchard. This cake is the first thing we bake with the fresh apples!

2 c. graham cracker crumbs
1/3 c. brown sugar, packed
1 stick butter, melted and
    divided
1 T. cinnamon
3 apples, peeled, cored and
    sliced into 12 rings
4 eggs

3/4 c. sugar
8 oz. ricotta cheese
8-oz. pkg. cream cheese,
    softened
2 t. vanilla extract
8 oz. whipping cream
Garnish: cinnamon

Combine cracker crumbs, brown sugar, 4 tablespoons butter and cinnamon. Press on bottom and part way up sides of a 9" springform pan. In a skillet, sauté the apple slices on both sides in the remaining 4 tablespoons of butter. Arrange 6 slices of apple on prepared crust. In a bowl, beat eggs, sugar, ricotta, cream cheese and vanilla until smooth. Add whipping cream and blend. Pour cheese mixture into pan over apple slices. Arrange the remaining 6 apple slices on top and press apples slightly under the mixture. Sprinkle top generously with cinnamon. Bake at 450 degrees for 10 minutes, then reduce heat to 300 degrees and bake for 50 to 55 minutes. Cool and refrigerate overnight.

The greatest medicine
is a true friend.

-Sir William Temple

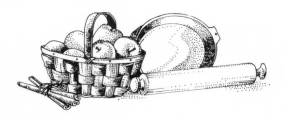

Maple-Walnut Pie

Lynda Robson
Boston, MA

After an afternoon spent raking leaves, jumping in them and raking them again; we love to come inside and enjoy a slice of this pie.

4 eggs, beaten
1-1/2 c. maple syrup
2 T. all-purpose flour
3 T. butter, melted and cooled
2 t. vanilla extract

3/4 c. walnuts, chopped
9-inch pie crust
Garnish: whipped cream and
  walnuts, crushed

In a large bowl, combine eggs and maple syrup. Beat in flour, butter and vanilla until well blended. Fold in walnuts and pour into the pie crust. Bake at 375 degrees for 35 minutes; pie filling will be soft when baked. Top with whipped cream and crushed nuts if desired.

Who will deny the truth? There is poetry in pies!

-Henry Wadsworth Longfellow

Bishop's Cake

Elizabeth VanEtten
Warwick, NY

It seems the name for this cake came about many years ago when the Bishop came to call on a family. They'd put out their best china, cloth napkins and he'd be served this special cake.

1 c. sugar
1/2 c. butter, softened
2 eggs, beaten
3 c. all-purpose flour

3 t. baking powder
1/2 t. salt
1 t. vanilla extract
1 c. milk

Beat together sugar, butter and eggs. In a separate bowl, combine flour, baking powder and salt. Mix the vanilla in with the milk. Slowly add dry ingredients to the creamed mixture alternately with the milk mixture. Pour cake mixture into a greased Bundt® pan. Prepare topping and sprinkle over cake mixture. Bake at 350 degrees for 30 to 45 minutes. The cake is done when it springs back with a light touch to the top. Cool several hours before removing to a cake plate.

Topping:

1 c. sugar
1 c. all-purpose flour
1 t. cinnamon

1 t. vanilla extract
1/2 c. butter, softened

Mix the sugar, flour, cinnamon and vanilla together. Cut in the butter until you have a mixture that resembles crumbs.

Don't put all your eggs in one basket!

-Italian proverb

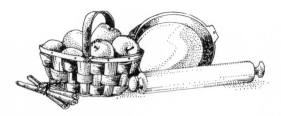

Luscious Blueberry Pie

Deborah Bassoff
Harrisburg, PA

*My grandmother was an expert baker and this recipe is considered
an heirloom in our family. You can purchase your pie crusts,
but try Grandma's recipe when time allows.*

2 pts. blueberries, washed and
   stems removed
1 c. sugar
2 T. all-purpose flour
1/8 t. cinnamon

1 T. lemon juice
1/8 t. salt
2 9-inch pie crusts
2 to 3 T. butter

Mix together first 6 ingredients. Line a 9" pie plate with bottom crust,
fill with blueberry filling and dot with butter. To prepare a lattice top,
roll out remaining crust and cut into long strips 1/2-inch in width. On
top of filled pie, make an "X" with 2 strips in the center of the pie.
Then, continue weaving strips allowing space between each strip in a
basket weave pattern. When completed, trim any edges and crimp the
lattice with the bottom crust. Bake at 425 degrees for 20 minutes then
lower the heat to 350 degrees and bake an additional 40 minutes.

Pie Crust for Two-Crust Pie:

2 c. all-purpose flour
1 t. salt

2/3 c. shortening
1/4 c. cold water

Mix together flour and salt; cut in shortening until mixture is the size
of peas. Blend in water until flour is moistened and shape into a ball.
Divide dough in half and roll out one at a time. If dough is too sticky,
keep flouring hands, board and rolling pin.

Vanilla Wafer Cake

Margie Scott
Winnsboro, TX

This is best enjoyed with good friends and coffee.

1 c. butter
2 c. sugar
6 eggs
12-oz. pkg. vanilla wafers,
    crushed

1 c. pecans, chopped
1/2 c. milk
1 t. vanilla extract

Cream butter and sugar together. Add eggs one at a time, beating after each. Add vanilla wafers, pecans, milk and vanilla. Pour into greased and floured Bundt® pan. Bake at 325 degrees for 1-1/2 hours; let cool before removing from pan.

If you're lucky enough to have some of Grandma's old-fashioned cake plates, get them out and enjoy them! They have beautiful patterns and will be a fond reminder of Grandma's wonderful desserts.

Grandma's Buttermilk Pie

Stephanie Mayer
Portsmouth, VA

Old-fashioned and simple.

1 stick butter
2 c. sugar
3 T. all-purpose flour
3 eggs, beaten

1 c. buttermilk
1 t. vanilla extract
1/8 t. nutmeg
9-inch pie crust

Cream butter and sugar together; beat in flour and eggs. Blend buttermilk, vanilla and nutmeg; stir into flour mixture. Spoon into pie crust and bake at 350 degrees for 45 to 50 minutes or until center is firm and set. Cool well before serving.

To bring a nostalgic feel to your kitchen, open a door on your pie safe to display your collection of heirloom kitchenware...butter molds and paddles, potato mashers, rolling pins, salt crocks and pie birds.

Banana-Nut Cake

Roberta Clark
Delaware, OH

Homemade applesauce is perfect served with this cake.

2-1/2 c. all-purpose flour
1-2/3 c. sugar
1-1/4 t. baking powder
1-1/4 t. baking soda
1 t. salt

2/3 c. shortening, softened
1-1/4 c. ripe bananas, mashed
2/3 c. buttermilk, divided
3 eggs
1 c. nuts, finely chopped

Blend flour, sugar, baking powder, baking soda and salt in mixing bowl. Add shortening, bananas and half of the buttermilk. Beat for 2 minutes at medium speed. Add remaining buttermilk and eggs, beating for 2 additional minutes, scraping bowl frequently. Fold in nuts and pour into two 8"x8" cake pans. Bake at 350 degrees for 35 to 40 minutes. Cool in pans for 5 minutes, then finish cooling on rack.

Pile everyone in the car and head out to a farmer's market! Bring home lots of just-picked berries, vegetables and bouquets of fresh flowers. It's a terrific way to spend Saturday morning.

Lemon Meringue Pie

Caroline Berman
Concord, MA

This recipe dates back to my great-grandmother. The memories I have of four generations of women in the kitchen are some of my fondest and have taught me the value of tradition. I cherish this heritage now and hope that my children will continue this tradition.

1 c. sugar
1 T. all-purpose flour
3 eggs, separated and divided
zest and juice of one lemon

milk
9-inch pie crust, baked
1/4 t. cream of tartar
2 T. powdered sugar

In heavy saucepan, stir together sugar, flour and egg yolks. Combine lemon zest and lemon juice in a one cup measuring cup. Add enough milk to equal one cup, then add to saucepan. Cook until thick, stirring often; pour into baked pie crust. Beat egg whites, cream of tartar and powdered sugar with electric mixer until the meringue is stiff and shiny. Spread over lemon filling. Be sure that meringue touches the inner edges of the crust so it doesn't pull away. Bake in a 350 degree oven for 10 to 15 minutes or until meringue is golden.

Some old-fashioned things like fresh air and sunshine are hard to beat. In our mad rush for progress... let's be sure we take along with us all the old-fashioned things worthwhile.

-Laura Ingalls Wilder

Chocolate-Buttermilk Cake

Carla Nelson
Newman Grove, NE

The best chocolate cake!

2 c. all-purpose flour
2 c. sugar
1 c. coffee or water
1/4 c. cocoa
2 sticks margarine

1/2 c. buttermilk
2 eggs
1 t. baking soda
1 t. vanilla extract

Combine flour and sugar in a large bowl. In saucepan, combine coffee or water, cocoa and margarine. Heat to boiling; stirring frequently. Pour boiling mixture over flour mixture. Add buttermilk, eggs, baking soda and vanilla. Mix well and pour into a 17-1/2"x11" jelly roll pan. Bake at 350 degrees for 20 minutes. Pour frosting over warm cake.

Frosting:

1/2 c. margarine
2 T. cocoa
1/4 c. cream

1/2 to 3/4 c. mini-
    marshmallows
3-1/2 c. powdered sugar
1 T. vanilla extract

Mix and heat margarine, cocoa and cream. After margarine is melted, add marshmallows and stir until melted. Beat in powdered sugar and vanilla.

Nutty Maple Pie

Cathy Hillier
Salt Lake City, UT

Rich and flavorful; a twist on traditional pecan pie.

2/3 c. sugar
6 T. unsalted butter, melted and
   cooled
4 eggs

1 c. maple syrup
1 c. whole hazelnuts, chopped
9-inch pie crust

Combine sugar, butter, eggs, maple syrup and hazelnuts. Pour into pie crust and bake at 400 degrees for 10 minutes; reduce heat to 325 degrees and bake an additional 25 minutes.

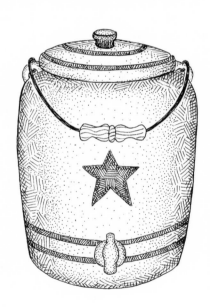

*If you're having a reunion or summertime picnic,
old-fashioned crocks with spigots are perfect!
Fill several with lemonade, milk, iced tea or
cider...guests can easily help themselves!*

Raspberry Upside-Down Cake

Becky Rogers
Saline, MI

Great served warm or cold and it couldn't be easier to prepare!

18-1/4 oz. box yellow cake mix
1 c. raspberries
3/4 c. sugar
1/2 c. whipping cream

Prepare cake mix according to package directions. Pour into two greased and floured 9" round cake pans. Place raspberries over top of cake mix. Sprinkle sugar over raspberries. Gently pour whipping cream over top. Bake for 25 to 35 minutes in a 350 degree oven. Let stand for 10 minutes. Turn upside down on plate to serve.

Nobby Apple Cake

Lynn Williams
Muncie, IN

This tasty recipe was found in a very old farmer's cookbook.

3 T. butter
1 c. sugar
1 egg, beaten
1/2 t. cinnamon
1/2 t. nutmeg
1/2 t. salt
1 t. baking soda
1 c. all-purpose flour
3 c. apples, peeled, cored and diced
1/4 c. nuts, chopped
1 t. vanilla extract

Cream together butter and sugar. Stir in egg until well blended. Sift together dry ingredients and add to butter mixture. Fold in apples and nuts; stir in vanilla. Pour into an oiled 8"x8" pan and bake at 350 degrees for 40 to 45 minutes.

To invite a person into your house is to take charge of his happiness for as long as he is under your roof.

-A. Brillat-Savarin

Raisin Pie

Cheri Maxwell
Gulf Breeze, FL

Grandma's favorite pie for taking to church socials!

3/4 c. sugar, divided
3 T. cornstarch
3 eggs, separated and divided
2 c. milk

1/2 c. raisins
2 t. lemon juice
9-inch pie crust, baked

Blend together 1/2 cup sugar and cornstarch. Transfer to a saucepan and stir in egg yolks and milk. Bring to a boil over medium heat and cook one minute. Remove saucepan from heat and stir in raisins and lemon juice; blending thoroughly. Spoon into pie crust; set aside. Using an electric mixer, beat egg whites until foamy, then slowly add remaining sugar, one tablespoon at a time, until egg whites become stiff. Spread meringue over pie filling, making sure it touches the edges of the pie crust. Bake at 350 degrees for 10 to 15 minutes or until lightly golden.

Use mini cookie cutters to make cut-outs from leftover pie crust dough. Bake at 350 degrees on an ungreased baking sheet until lightly golden. They look pretty sprinkled around the edges of a pie plate or on top of individual slices.

Harvest Pumpkin Cake

Tina Wery
Junction City, KS

*Try serving this with a dollop of whipped cream
and a sprinkle of fresh nutmeg.*

3 c. all-purpose flour
2 t. baking powder
2 t. baking soda
1 t. salt
3-1/2 t. cinnamon

4 eggs
2 c. sugar
1-1/2 c. oil
16-oz. can pumpkin
1 c. walnuts, chopped

Sift together dry ingredients. In large bowl, beat eggs, gradually adding sugar, beat until thick. Beating constantly, add oil. Continue beating at low speed, alternate dry ingredients and pumpkin ending with dry ingredients; fold in nuts. Pour batter into greased Bundt® pan. Bake at 350 degrees for approximately one hour or until inserted toothpick comes out clean. Cool cake for 10 minutes in pan and turn onto serving platter; cool completely. Dust cake with sifted powdered sugar if desired.

*Dough bowls bring a nostalgic feel to a kitchen.
Filled with fruit or herb bundles, they bring back
memories and scents of Grandma's house.*

Company Special Gooseberry Pie

Carol Richardson
Independence, MO

My dear mother passed this recipe on to me and over the years I've tried several gooseberry pie recipes; this is the best by far...I can guarantee it to be a good one.

3 c. fresh gooseberries, divided
1-1/2 c. sugar
3 T. quick-cooking tapioca
1/8 t. salt

2 9-inch pie crusts
2 T. butter
1 T. milk

In medium-size saucepan, crush one cup gooseberries; add sugar, dry tapioca and salt. Stir in remainder of berries; cook, stirring constantly until thick. Pour into pie crust; dot with butter. Cover with top crust; seal edges. Cut several small vents in the top crust and brush with milk. Bake at 425 degrees for 35 to 45 minutes, or until golden brown. Cool before serving.

Country life has its conveniences...there is a delicious smell everywhere...and the gooseberries are growing.

-Anton Chekov

Shoo Fly Pie

Shelley Turner
Boise, ID

This wonderful brown sugar and molasses pie is such an old-fashioned favorite...so warm and sweet!

3/4 c. corn syrup
1/4 c. molasses
1 c. hot water
1 t. baking soda
1 egg

1 c. all-purpose flour
1 T. butter
1 t. vanilla extract
2/3 c. brown sugar, packed
9-inch pie crust

Blend together corn syrup, molasses, water, baking soda and egg; set aside half. To the remaining half, stir in flour, butter, vanilla and brown sugar, mixing until well blended. Pour into pie crust and spoon reserved molasses mixture over pie filling. Bake at 400 degrees for 25 minutes. Cool well before serving.

An old-fashioned pie and cake auction makes a great fund raiser! Place pies and cakes in decorated boxes and let the fun begin!

Smokey Hollow Pound Cake

Kathy Matthews
Sanford, NC

*We enjoy this pound cake with strawberries and whipped cream.
My mother-in-law butters a slice and then places under
the broiler to toast; great for breakfast, too!*

8-oz. pkg. cream cheese	6 eggs
2 sticks margarine	3 c. cake flour
1/2 c. shortening	1-1/2 t. lemon extract
3 c. sugar	1 t. vanilla extract

In a bowl combine cream cheese, margarine and shortening; mix until creamy. Add sugar; blend well. Stir in eggs and cake flour. Using an electric mixer on low speed, blend in lemon and vanilla extracts. When thoroughly combined, pour into a greased and floured 10" tube pan. Bake at 325 degrees for one hour and 15 minutes.

*If you're short on cake flour
for a recipe, you can
substitute one cup of
all-purpose flour, minus
2 tablespoons... a last minute
substitution that equals
one cup of cake flour!*

Nana's Cheese Pie

Susie Knupp
Bailey, CO

I can remember 40 years ago when my sister-in-law and I ate too much of this pie at a family get-together! My mother-in-law always made 3 or 4 different kinds of pie, but this one was everyone's favorite and for the last 4 generations, it's been the most requested recipe in our family.

1-1/2 c. graham cracker crumbs
1/3 c. plus 1/2 c. plus 3 T. sugar,
   divided
1/3 c. butter, melted

3 8-oz. pkgs. cream cheese,
   softened
2 eggs, separated and divided
1/2 pt. sour cream

Combine cracker crumbs, 1/3 cup sugar and butter together in a bowl; reserve 2 tablespoons. Press crust into an 8" or 9" pie pan; set aside. Beat cream cheese, 1/2 cup sugar and egg yolks until smooth. Beat egg whites until stiff and fold in gently. Pour into crust and bake at 325 degrees for 20 minutes; cool. Mix sour cream and remaining 3 tablespoons sugar and pour over cooled pie. Sprinkle with reserved graham cracker crumbs.

There is nothing wrong with the world that a sensible woman could not settle in an afternoon.

-Jean Giraudoux

Root Beer Cake

Tish DeYoung
Wausau, WI

Yes, it sounds unusual, but it's wonderful!

1 c. sugar
1/2 c. butter
1/2 t. vanilla extract
2 eggs

2 c. all-purpose flour
1 T. baking powder
1 t. salt
2/3 c. root beer

Combine all ingredients in a large mixing bowl. Blend at low speed; beat for 3 minutes at medium speed. Pour into greased and floured 12"x8" pan. Bake at 375 degrees for 30 to 35 minutes. Apply frosting to cooled cake.

Frosting:

1 lb. powdered sugar

1 c. root beer, chilled

Combine in mixer bowl and blend well. Beat until thick and fluffy.

A great activity for family night... make your own root beer! Root beer extract can be found at your grocery store, just follow the easy directions on the bottle and enjoy!

Kentucky Pie

Jan Kerth
Cincinnati, OH

Growing up I spent most of my summers in Kentucky on my grandparents' farm. I especially remember my grandmother's cooking; she was always baking a pie. This was my favorite; very rich and very southern. Now, when I bake it, it brings back many wonderful memories.

1 stick margarine
2 c. sugar
1 T. cornstarch
3 eggs

1 c. evaporated milk
1 t. vanilla extract
9-inch pie crust

Melt margarine; stir in sugar and cornstarch. Add eggs, one at a time, beating well after each one. Add milk and vanilla; stir well. Pour into pie crust. Bake at 350 degrees for 50 to 60 minutes. Refrigerate for several hours before serving.

Baking pies for 100 of your closest friends. . . you'll need 13 pies and 4 gallons of ice cream to top them off!

Orange Meringue Pie

Patricia Wesson
Westminster, CO

*A light pie, great after dinner when you want just a
little something sweet, but not heavy.*

1 c. orange juice
1 c. orange sections, chopped
2 T. orange zest
1 c. plus 6 T. sugar, divided
5 T. cornstarch
3 egg yolks, beaten

2 T. lemon juice
2 T. butter
9-inch pie crust, baked
4 egg whites, room temperature
1/4 t. salt
1/2 t. vanilla extract

Combine orange juice, orange sections, orange zest, one cup sugar
and cornstarch. Cook over low heat until mixture becomes clear. Add
a little of the hot mixture to egg yolks and stir. Return egg yolks to hot
mixture and cook about 5 minutes longer; remove from heat. Blend in
lemon juice and butter. Pour into warm pie crust. To prepare meringue,
place egg whites in a mixing bowl, then place that bowl into a larger
bowl of hot water. Stir constantly until the whites feel warm, then
add salt and vanilla. Remove bowl from the hot water and beat in
remaining sugar, one tablespoon at a time with an electric mixer.
Continue to beat until the meringue is stiff and shiny. Cover filling
with meringue, touching edges of crust. Bake for 15 to 20 minutes
in a 350 degree oven or until lightly golden.

*A homemade friend wears
longer than one
you buy in the market.*

-Austin O'Malley

Moon Cake

Cindy VanNatta
Platteville, WI

This recipe makes a very pretty all-white cake that puffs up!

1/2 c. butter
1 c. boiling water
1 c. all-purpose flour
4 eggs
3 3-1/2 oz. pkgs. instant vanilla
    pudding mix

5 c. milk
8-oz. pkg. cream cheese
Garnish: whipped topping and
    chocolate bar, shaved

Place butter in a 3-quart saucepan and add water. Heat to boiling and stir until butter is melted. Add flour all at once to boiling mixture, stirring constantly until mixture leaves side of pan and forms a ball. Remove from heat and cool. Add eggs, one at a time, and beat until very smooth; batter will be thick. Spread in an oiled 13"x9" baking pan and bake at 350 degrees for 30 to 40 minutes. Prepare pudding using 5 cups of milk, add cream cheese and beat until smooth. Spread on top of cooled cake. Top with whipped topping and sprinkle chocolate shavings on top.

Any cake is beautiful topped with edible flowers...violets, rose petals, lilies, forget-me-nots, pansies, nasturtiums and Johnny-jump-ups. Be sure to use only organic flowers and wash them well.

Mississippi Mud Cake

Gail Goudy
Walls, MS

Rich and chocolatey!

2 sticks margarine	1-1/3 c. all-purpose flour
1/2 c. cocoa	1/4 t. salt
4 eggs, beaten	1 t. vanilla extract
2 c. sugar	2 c. mini-marshmallows

Melt margarine and cocoa over low heat; cool. Add eggs and sugar, mixing well. Stir in flour, salt and vanilla. Bake in a 13"x9" pan at 325 degrees for 35 minutes. Upon removing from oven, cover with marshmallows and brown lightly; pour topping over marshmallows.

Topping:

1/2 stick margarine	1/2 c. milk
1/3 c. cocoa	16-oz. box powdered sugar

Mix margarine, cocoa and milk; bring to a boil and continue boiling for one minute. Remove from heat and add powdered sugar.

Tuck a jar of homemade pie filling, favorite pie recipe and a pie bird in a pretty pie plate...a tasty and welcome gift!

Walnut & Rome Apple Cake

Denise Cechvala
Ford City, PA

For a pretty presentation, just tuck inside a vintage apple basket!

3 eggs, beaten
1-3/4 c. sugar
1 c. oil
1 t. baking soda
1/4 t. salt
1 to 2 t. cinnamon

2 c. all-purpose flour
4 c. Rome apples, peeled, cored
　　and chopped
1 c. walnuts, chopped
Garnish: powdered sugar

Beat eggs and sugar for 5 minutes, or until sugar has dissolved and mixture is thick. Keep beating and add oil, baking soda, salt and cinnamon. Slowly add flour until batter is smooth and thick. Stir in apples and walnuts. Pour batter in a greased 13"x9" pan and bake at 350 degrees for one hour. Let cool and sprinkle with powdered sugar.

If you don't have time to frost a cake, you can give it an extra-special look in no time! Just lay a cake stencil over the top of a cooled cake...they come in all kinds of pretty patterns. Sprinkle on powdered sugar or cocoa, then gently remove the stencil to show your pattern.

Raspberry Crunch Cheesecake

*Debi Timperley
Stanton, NE*

Make this the night before; a great time saver!

2 c. quick-cooking oatmeal
2 c. brown sugar, packed
2 c. all-purpose flour
1 c. butter
1 c. nuts, chopped
2-1/2 lbs. cream cheese

1 c. sugar
1/4 c. cornstarch
1/2 c. cream
4 eggs
10-oz. jar seedless raspberry
   jam

In a bowl, mix together oatmeal, brown sugar and flour. Cut in the butter to make crumbs; add nuts. Press 3/4 of mixture into the bottom and halfway up the sides of a greased 10" springform pan. Bake at 350 degrees for 12 to 15 minutes to set crust. Save the remaining crumbs for the top of cake. In a large bowl, with an electric mixer, beat the cream cheese, sugar, cornstarch and cream. Add eggs, one at a time, beating well after each. Pour into prebaked crust-lined pan. Bake at 350 degrees for 45 minutes. Heat jam in microwave, then pour over the hot cake and top with reserved crumbs. Return to oven and bake for 15 to 20 minutes, or until the crust is a golden brown. Turn off oven and let the cake set in the oven for one hour. Chill overnight.

*The whole worth of a
kind deed lies in the love
that inspires it.*

-The Talmud

Fudge Cake

Jane Fleming
Elkview, WV

*If you're craving chocolate, try this! The peanut
butter gives it a special taste.*

2 c. all-purpose flour
2 c. sugar
3 sticks margarine, divided
8 T. cocoa, divided
1 c. water
1/2 c. buttermilk
2 eggs
1 t. baking soda

1/2 t. cinnamon
2 t. vanilla extract, divided
1 c. peanut butter
1 t. oil
5 T. milk
16-oz. box powdered sugar
2 4-oz. pkgs. chopped nuts

Sift together flour and sugar; set aside. In a saucepan, mix 2 sticks
margarine, 4 tablespoons cocoa and water; bring to a rapid boil and let
cool. Pour cocoa mixture over flour mixture; beat. Add buttermilk,
eggs, baking soda, cinnamon and one teaspoon vanilla. Beat after
every addition. Pour mixture into a greased and floured 13"x9" glass
baking dish. Bake at 350 degrees for 25 to 30 minutes; let cool. Mix
peanut butter and oil; spread on cooled cake. Place in refrigerator until
peanut butter is chilled. In saucepan, mix remaining margarine, cocoa
and milk. Boil for 2 minutes; remove from heat. Beat in powdered
sugar, remaining vanilla and nuts. Spread over cooled cake.

*Keep a peg rack in your
kitchen for hanging pot
holders, oven mitts,
dish cloths and aprons!*

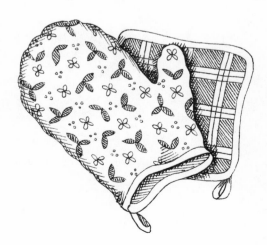

Apple-Dapple Pie

Tami Bowman
Gooseberry Patch

*Serve slices warm with a spoonful of whipped cream
and a sprinkle of nutmeg on top.*

2 T. crushed pineapple
14-1/2 oz. can cherry pie filling
2 c. apples, peeled, cored and
    sliced
2 T. tapioca
1 T. cornstarch

3/4 c. sugar
1/4 t. cinnamon
1/8 t. nutmeg
1 t. butter, softened
9-inch pie crust

In a large bowl, blend together pineapple, cherry pie filling and apples.
Sift together dry tapioca, cornstarch, sugar, cinnamon and nutmeg.
Stir into pineapple mixture and blend in butter. Pour into pie crust and
bake at 400 degrees for 10 minutes, reduce heat to 375 degrees and
bake for an additional 20 minutes.

*Good apple pies are a considerable part of our
domestic happiness.*

-Jane Austen

Praline-Cream Cheese Pound Cake

Vicki Jones
Rutherfordton, NC

My favorite because it has a rich caramel flavor that satisfies my most urgent sweet tooth!

2 sticks butter, softened
8-oz. pkg. cream cheese
1 lb. brown sugar
1 c. sugar
5 eggs

3-1/2 c. cake flour
1/2 t. baking powder
1 c. milk
1-1/2 t. vanilla extract
1 c. pecans, chopped

Cream butter and cream cheese together. Add brown sugar and sugar, one cup at a time, beating until light and fluffy. Add eggs, one at a time, beating well after each. Sift flour and baking powder together and add to creamed mixture alternately with milk, beginning and ending with flour. Add vanilla and nuts; mix well. Pour into a greased and floured tube pan. Bake at 300 degrees for 2 hours or until tests done. Cool in pan for 10 minutes, remove from pan and cool on wire rack. Spread with frosting.

Frosting:

3 c. sugar, divided
1/2 c. water
1 egg, beaten
1 c. milk

1 stick butter
1 t. vinegar
1/8 t. salt

Place 1/2 cup of sugar in a heavy skillet. Cook over low heat, stirring constantly until melted and brown. Add water and stir until dissolved. Add remaining sugar. Mix egg with milk and stir into sugar mixture. Add butter, vinegar and salt. Cook to soft ball stage, 234 to 240 degrees on candy thermometer; cool. Beat until reaches spreading consistency.

Peanut Butter Strudel Pie

Phyllis Laughrey
Mt. Vernon, OH

The best peanut butter pie! Topped with meringue, it's wonderful!

1/4 c. peanut butter
3/4 c. powdered sugar
9-inch pie crust, baked
1/2 c. all-purpose flour
2/3 c. plus 1/2 c. sugar, divided
1/4 t. salt

2 c. milk, scalded
3 eggs, separated and divided
2 T. butter
1/2 t. vanilla extract
1/4 t. cream of tartar
1 t. cornstarch

Mix peanut butter and powdered sugar together by hand, until crumbly. Spread over bottom of pie crust, reserving about one tablespoon for topping. Mix flour, 2/3 cup sugar and salt; gradually add milk. Cook over medium heat until mixture thickens and boils, about 2 minutes. Remove from heat and set aside. Beat egg yolks and blend in a small amount of milk mixture; stir well. Return to pan and cook for one minute. Add butter and vanilla; cool. Pour over peanut butter crumbs in pie crust. Beat egg whites until firm; add cream of tartar and beat until thick. Add 1/2 cup sugar and cornstarch; beat until stiff. Spoon on top of pie. Be sure to seal the edges with the meringue to avoid spillover of pie contents. Bake at 425 degrees until delicately brown. Cool and serve.

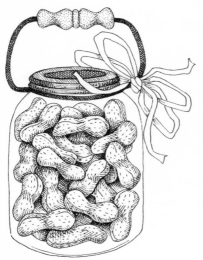

*Where there are friends,
there is wealth.*

-Plautus

Cookie Dough Cheesecake

Valarie Dobbins
Edmond, OK

Who can resist cookie dough? Indulge in this!

1-3/4 c. chocolate chip cookie crumbs
1-1/2 c. sugar, divided
1/3 c. plus 1/4 c. butter, melted and divided
3 8-oz. pkgs. cream cheese, softened
3 eggs

8 oz. sour cream
1-1/2 t. vanilla extract, divided
1/4 c. brown sugar, packed
1 T. water
1/2 c. all-purpose flour
1-1/2 c. mini semi-sweet chocolate chips, divided

In a small bowl, combine cookie crumbs and 1/4 cup sugar; stir in 1/3 cup butter. Press into bottom and slightly up the sides of a greased 9" springform pan; set aside. In a mixing bowl, beat cream cheese and one cup sugar until smooth. Add eggs; beat on low just until combined. Add sour cream and 1/2 teaspoon vanilla; beat just until blended. Pour over crust; set aside. In a separate mixing bowl, cream remaining butter and sugars on medium speed for 3 minutes; add water and remaining vanilla; gradually add flour and stir in one cup chocolate chips. Drop by teaspoonfuls over filling, gently pushing dough below surface. Bake at 350 degrees for 45 to 55 minutes or until center is almost set. Cool on a wire rack for 10 minutes. Carefully run a knife around the edge of pan to loosen; cool one hour longer. Refrigerate overnight, then remove sides of pan and sprinkle with remaining chips.

Milk served in vintage pint-size milk bottles adds fun to family dessert time!

123

Very Berry Pie

Tori Willis
Champaign, IL

All of my favorite fruits are in this juicy pie!

5-1/2 c. plus 2/3 c. all-purpose
    flour, divided
1/4 t. salt
2 c. shortening
1 egg
1 T. vinegar
3/4 c. cold water
2 c. blueberries

2 c. raspberries
2 c. strawberries, sliced
2 c. rhubarb, chopped
4 c. apples, peeled, cored and
    chopped
2 c. sugar
2 T. lemon juice

Sift 5-1/2 cups of flour and salt together; cut in shortening. Whisk together egg, vinegar and cold water and stir into dry ingredients. Separate dough into 4 sections. Cover each with plastic wrap and refrigerate for 30 minutes. Remove pastry from refrigerator, one section at a time, and roll out to a 9-inch circle; place one pastry circle in the bottom of each 9" pie pan. Stir together fruit, sugar, remaining flour and lemon juice and spoon half into pie crust. Roll a second portion of pastry into a 9-inch circle and place over filling. Seal edges and cut slits in top of crust to vent steam; repeat with remaining portions of dough and fruit filling. Bake at 350 degrees for 50 to 60 minutes. Makes 2 pies.

Cobblers & Bread Puddings

Raisin Bread Pudding

Janice Roebuck
North Judson, IN

When it comes to comfort food, this is the best!

1/2 loaf of white bread, torn
6 c. milk
5 eggs, beaten
1 T. cinnamon
1-1/2 c. brown sugar, packed
1 c. raisins

cinnamon and sugar to taste
1 c. sugar
2 T. cornstarch
2 c. boiling water
2 t. vanilla extract
4 T. butter

Place bread into a greased 13"x9" pan. In a large bowl, blend milk, eggs, cinnamon, brown sugar and raisins. Mix well and pour over the bread; sprinkle with a mixture of cinnamon and sugar. Bake at 350 degrees for 1-1/2 to 2 hours, or until golden brown. In saucepan, combine sugar and cornstarch. Gradually stir in boiling water, bring to a boil and continue boiling for one minute, stirring constantly. Add vanilla extract and butter, stir until butter is melted. Pour vanilla sauce over slices of cooled bread.

Take time to laugh, it's the music of the soul.

-Anonymous

Apple Pandowdy

Vickie

An old favorite...everyone should try this!

4 tart apples, peeled, cored and
    sliced
1/2 t. cinnamon
1/2 c. molasses
5 T. butter, divided

2-1/3 c. biscuit baking mix
1/2 c. milk
3 T. sugar
Garnish: whipped topping and
    nutmeg

Place apples in a buttered 9" pie plate; sprinkle with cinnamon. Drizzle
molasses over cinnamon and dot with 2 tablespoons butter. Stir
together biscuit baking mix, milk and sugar. Melt remaining butter and
blend into biscuit mixture. Knead biscuit dough 10 times and roll out
to 1/2-inch thick. Lay dough over apple mixture and cut steam vents.
Bake at 375 degrees for 30 minutes. Spoon into bowls and garnish
with whipped topping and nutmeg.

*Strands of dried apple
slices make a folky
and fragrant garland.
Drape it across your
mantel, window or
slide several slices on
a wire; then shape
into a heart.*

Cherry Cobbler

Karen Hess
Scott City, KS

*One of my favorites because it seems just right after a meal;
it's not too sweet and it takes very little time to prepare.*

1 c. cherries, drained, reserving
   juice
1/2 c. plus 1-1/2 T. sugar,
   divided
1 c. plus 1 T. all-purpose flour,
   divided

1/4 t. plus 1/8 t. salt, divided
1/4 t. almond extract
red food coloring
1-1/2 t. baking powder
3 T. margarine
1/3 c. milk

Spray an 8"x8" baking pan with non-stick spray. Place cherries in pan;
set aside. Heat cherry juice, 1/2 cup sugar, one tablespoon flour and
1/8 teaspoon salt. Cook, stirring constantly, for 2 minutes. Add
almond extract and a few drops of food coloring; pour over cherries.
Sift remaining flour with remaining salt, baking powder and remaining
sugar. Blend in margarine until crumbly; stir in milk. Drop by
tablespoonfuls over cherry mixture; brush with milk and sprinkle
with sugar to taste. Bake for 15 to 20 minutes at 425 degrees.

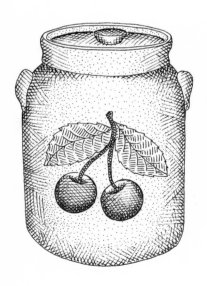

*Give new neighbors a break
from unpacking and surprise
them with a still-warm
cobbler from your oven. Take
along some plates, forks,
napkins and a pitcher of cold
milk. . . a tasty treat!*

Lemony Bread Pudding

Linda Staley
Ashley, OH

A yummy comfort food topped with lemon sauce.

2 c. dry bread, cubed
4 c. milk, scalded
3 T. butter, divided
1/4 t. plus 1/8 t. salt, divided
1-1/4 c. sugar, divided
4 eggs, beaten

1 t. vanilla extract
1 T. cornstarch
1/8 t. nutmeg
1 c. boiling water
1-1/2 T. lemon juice

Soak bread in hot milk for 5 minutes. Add one tablespoon butter, 1/4 teaspoon salt and 3/4 cup sugar. Pour mixture over eggs, add vanilla and mix well. Spoon into a greased 2-quart baking dish. Set baking dish in a larger pan filled with hot water and bake at 350 degrees for 50 minutes or until firm. Mix remaining sugar, cornstarch, remaining salt and nutmeg; gradually add water. Cook over low heat until thick and clear. Add remaining butter and lemon juice; blend thoroughly. Serve over bread pudding.

My very best friends are those who know
without ever being told.

-Authine Steinbeck

Blueberry Buckle

Karen Bernards
San Fernando, CA

A great treat at breakfast or any time of the day...my family loves it!

1-1/4 c. sugar, divided
1/2 c. butter, softened and
  divided
1 egg
1/2 c. milk

2-1/3 c. all-purpose flour,
  divided
2 t. baking powder
1/2 t. salt
2 c. blueberries
1/2 t. cinnamon

Mix 3/4 cup sugar, 1/4 cup butter and egg; stir in milk. Sift together 2 cups flour, baking powder and salt; add to batter. Blend in blueberries. Spread batter into a greased 9"x9" pan. In medium bowl, combine remaining sugar, flour, butter and cinnamon. Place crumb topping over blueberry mixture. Bake at 375 degrees for 35 to 40 minutes. Makes 9 servings.

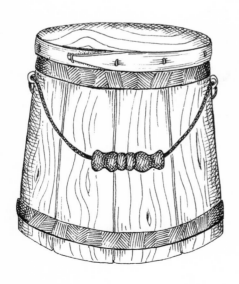

Enjoy the simple pleasures of life... slipping into flannel sheets on a cold winter's night, the smell of fresh-cut grass, the sound of children at play, a good laugh!

Creamy Pear Bread Pudding

Tori Willis
Champaign, IL

*Pears and bread pudding are two of my favorites; so I came
up with this recipe that combines the best of both!*

1 t. rum extract
1 t. water
1/2 c. raisins
1 T. butter
2 c. pears, peeled and sliced
1/2 c. sugar, divided

4 c. white bread, torn
3 c. milk, scalded
3 eggs, beaten
1 t. vanilla extract
1 c. whipping cream

In a small saucepan, blend together rum extract and water. Heat just
to boiling and pour over raisins. Melt butter in saucepan; stir in pear
slices and sauté for 5 minutes. Stir in 1/4 cup sugar and continue to
cook for 2 minutes. Place bread in a buttered 2-quart baking dish,
pour milk in and let soak 5 minutes. Fold in raisin and pear mixtures.
Thoroughly combine eggs, remaining sugar, vanilla and cream;
combine with bread mixture. Bake at 350 degrees for 50 minutes.

Rhubarb Heaven

Laura Greenfield
Mansfield, MA

This couldn't be easier to make!

4 c. rhubarb, chopped
1 c. sugar
18-1/4 oz. box white cake mix

3-oz. pkg. strawberry gelatin
1 c. water
1/3 c. butter, melted

Place first 4 ingredients in a 13"x9" pan in the order listed; the cake
mix and gelatin go in dry. Add water and butter on the top; don't stir.
Bake at 350 degrees for 45 to 60 minutes.

Blackberry Cobbler

*Diane Long
Delaware, OH*

A great recipe for all those fresh, juicy summer berries!

1 stick butter
1 c. all-purpose flour
1 c. milk
1-1/3 c. sugar, divided
2 t. baking powder

2 T. cornstarch
2 t. lemon juice
1/4 t. nutmeg
1/2 t. cinnamon
2 c. blackberries

Melt butter in an 8"x8" baking dish. Blend together flour, milk, one cup sugar and baking powder; pour batter into dish. Mix together remaining ingredients and pour into center of batter; don't stir. Bake at 375 degrees for 45 minutes.

Do not wait for extraordinary circumstances to do good actions: try to use ordinary situations.

-Jean Paul Richter

Cinnamon Bread Pudding

Sharon Gould
Howard City, MI

*The cinnamon bread makes this pudding extra special, and
the warm butter sauce is so good drizzled over top!*

6 eggs
2 c. milk
2 c. half-and-half, divided
1 c. sugar
2 t. vanilla extract

6 c. cinnamon bread, cubed
1/2 c. brown sugar, packed
1/4 c. butter
1/2 c. corn syrup

In large mixing bowl, whisk eggs; blend in milk, 1-3/4 cups of half-and-half, sugar and vanilla until combined. Stir in bread cubes until lightly moistened. Grease a 2-quart rectangular baking dish and spread mixture in evenly. Bake at 325 degrees for 55 to 60 minutes, or until center starts to firm. In small saucepan, heat brown sugar and butter until butter is melted. Carefully, add corn syrup and remaining half-and-half. Cook, stirring constantly over medium-low heat for one to 2 minutes or until sugar dissolves and mixture is smooth. Serve over warm pudding.

*A memory quilt
will always remind you of dear
friends. Gather everyone together
and have each person trace
her handprint on homespun,
cut out, then appliqué handprints
on squares of muslin. Ask friends
to sign or write a message on
the muslin before stitching the
blocks together.*

Pumpkin Crisp

Judy Wilson
Hutchinson, MN

*Everyone comes together at dinnertime when they
know there's pumpkin crisp for dessert!*

16-oz. can pumpkin
12-oz. can evaporated milk
1 c. sugar
2 t. cinnamon
3 eggs
18-1/4 oz. box yellow cake mix

1-1/2 c. pecans, chopped
2 sticks margarine, melted
8-oz. pkg. cream cheese,
  softened
1/2 c. powdered sugar
3/4 c. whipped topping

Mix pumpkin, milk, sugar, cinnamon and eggs together with mixer
until well blended. Pour into greased 13"x9" pan. Sprinkle dry cake
mix over the top, then sprinkle pecans over cake mix; drizzle
margarine over all; don't stir. Bake at 350 degrees for one hour. Cool
and invert on a large platter. Blend together cream cheese, powdered
sugar and whipped topping and spread over cooled crisp. Makes 10 to
12 servings.

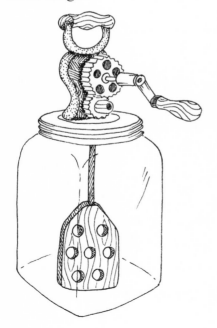

*Taking your cobbler to a family
get-together? Keep it warm in a
cobbler cozy. Lay two place mats
together; wrong sides out.
Stitch three sides together,
leaving one of the short ends
open. Turn right side out and
your baking dish will slip
inside. Secure the ends with
strips of fastening tape.*

Chocolate Lover's Bread Pudding   *Jo Ann*

*What a combination! An old-fashioned comfort food combined
with chocolate...it's a chocolate lover's dream!*

4 bread slices, crusts removed
1 oz. unsweetened chocolate,
   chopped
4 c. milk

2 eggs, beaten
1 c. sugar
1 t. vanilla extract

Tear bread into bite-size pieces and place in a small saucepan. Stir in
chocolate and milk and bring to a boil, stirring constantly. Remove
from heat. Blend eggs and sugar together and gradually pour milk
mixture over eggs, constantly stirring. Mix in vanilla and pour into a
2-quart casserole dish. Place casserole dish in a larger pan filled with
water. Bake at 350 degrees for one hour or until a knife inserted in the
center comes out clean.

*We dare not trust our wit for making our house pleasant
to our friend, so we buy ice cream.*

-Ralph Waldo Emerson

Cookie Cobbler

Donna Dye
London, OH

So easy, even when you're short on time!

16-oz. can whole cranberry
  sauce
1/3 c. brown sugar, packed
3 T. all-purpose flour
1 t. cinnamon

4 apples, peeled, cored, sliced
  and halved
1/2 of an 18-oz. pkg.
  refrigerated sugar cookie
  dough

Blend together cranberry sauce, brown sugar, flour and cinnamon in a mixing bowl; fold in apples and stir. Spread cobbler filling in the bottom of a 13"x9" baking dish. Slice cookie dough into 1/4-inch slices and lay over filling. Bake at 400 degrees for 30 to 35 minutes or until apples are tender.

Use florist wire to attach measuring spoons, cookie cutters, child-size rolling pins and wooden spoons on a circle of grapevine...a whimsical kitchen wreath!

Cobblers & Bread Puddings

Just Peachy Bread Pudding

Erin Doell
Glen Ellyn, IL

Serve this with a big scoop of cinnamon ice cream!

1 loaf French bread, cubed
16-oz. can sliced peaches,
   drained
1/2 c. raisins
4 eggs, separated and divided
3/4 c. sugar

12-oz. can evaporated milk
2 c. milk
1/2 t. cinnamon
1/4 t. nutmeg
1 t. coconut extract
1 T. vanilla extract

Fill a buttered 3-quart baking dish with bread cubes, peach slices and raisins; stir gently and set aside. Combine 2 eggs and 2 egg whites with sugar, reserving remaining yolks for another use. Stir together evaporated milk, milk, spices, coconut and vanilla extracts and egg mixture; blend. Pour egg mixture evenly over bread, gently stirring to coat. Bake at 350 degrees for 30 to 40 minutes or until a knife inserted near the center comes out clean.

Make your own recipe cards by stenciling or rubber stamping unlined 6"x4" index cards. Add a checkerboard border, apples or sunflowers; then tie several together with strands of raffia.

Plum Kuchen

Patricia Wesson
Westminster, CO

*After placing on serving plates, I like to drizzle a little
cream on top of each slice...yummy!*

1-1/4 c. all-purpose flour
1/2 c. sugar, divided
1-1/2 t. baking powder
1/2 c. butter, divided
1 egg
1/4 c. milk
1 t. vanilla extract

2 lbs. plums, cut in half and
    quartered
1 t. cinnamon
1/3 c. strawberry preserves
1 T. water
Garnish: vanilla ice cream or
    whipped cream

Grease a 13"x9" baking dish. In medium bowl, sift flour with 1/4 cup
sugar and baking powder. Using a fork, cut in 1/4 cup butter until
mixture resembles coarse crumbs. Beat egg slightly with a fork, then
add milk and vanilla; blend well. Add to flour mixture, beating vigor-
ously until smooth, about one minute. Batter will be quite stiff. Using
spatula or rubber scraper, spread batter evenly in bottom of prepared
baking dish. Arrange plum slices over batter, slightly overlapping, in
rows. Place extra slices between rows. Mix remaining sugar,
cinnamon and butter; spoon over fruit. Bake at 400 degrees for
35 minutes or until fruit is tender and pastry is golden. Remove to
wire rack to cool slightly. In small saucepan, over medium heat, mix
strawberry preserves with water, stirring until preserves are melted;
brush over fruit. Serve warm with ice cream or whipped cream.

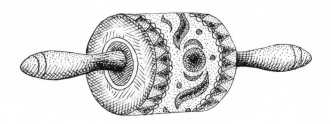

Cheese and bread make the cheeks red!

-German proverb

Raspberry Cobbler

Kathy McGuire
Wenonah, NJ

Perfect if you're short on time; it's quick to make and delicious!

1 c. all-purpose flour
1/4 c. plus 1/2 T. sugar, divided
1/8 t. salt
1 stick unsalted butter, chilled
and cut into pieces
1-1/2 T. ice water

2 10-oz. pkgs. whole frozen,
unsweetened raspberries
2 T. whipping cream
Garnish: whipped cream

Prepare dough by combining flour, 1/2 tablespoon sugar and salt in a medium bowl. Cut in the butter until the mixture resembles coarse meal. Add water, a few drops at a time, just enough to hold dough together. Place the pastry on a lightly floured board and roll into a rectangle 1/8-inch thick; chill for 20 minutes. Place the raspberries in the bottom of an 11"x7" baking dish. Sprinkle evenly with remaining sugar; place the dough over the raspberries; crimp edges. Cut steam vents in dough, brush with cream and sprinkle with the remaining sugar. Bake cobbler at 425 degrees for 25 minutes or until the pastry is golden brown and the fruit juices are bubbling in the center. Serve warm with whipped cream.

The man who is loved by the house cat, by the dog, by the neighbor's children, and by his own wife, is a great man, even if he has never had his name in "Who's Who".

-Thomas Dreier

Texas-Style Bread Pudding

Corrine Lane
Marysville, OH

There's just something sweet and warming about bread pudding.

2 T. butter
6 bread slices
2 Red Delicious or Cortland
    apples, peeled, cored and
    coarsely chopped
3 T. raisins
1/4 c. walnuts, chopped

2 eggs, beaten
2/3 c. sugar
1-1/2 c. whipping cream
1 c. apple cider
1-1/2 t. cinnamon
1/2 t. nutmeg

Evenly butter one side of each slice of bread and cut slices diagonally into 4 pieces. Lay 8 bread sections in the bottom of 2-quart casserole dish. Divide chopped apples into 4 equal amounts, then alternate layers of apples, then bread; repeat 2 more times. Toss together raisins and walnuts and place over bread layer. Top with remaining apple pieces. Blend eggs and sugar; stir in cream, apple cider, cinnamon and nutmeg. Pour over top of bread mixture; don't stir. Cover casserole dish and bake at 350 degrees for 40 to 50 minutes or until a knife inserted in the center comes out clean.

If you're going to a potluck, serve this bread pudding up Texas-style! Wrap your casserole dish in a red bandanna and tuck it in a denim-lined basket. Be sure to include recipe cards rubber stamped with stars or boots!

Persimmon Crisp

Rosalie Benson
Martinez, CA

*Beginning with a recipe that used apples, I made some
changes and created this tasty persimmon crisp!*

6 c. ripe persimmons, sliced
1-1/4 t. cinnamon
1/4 t. nutmeg
3/4 c. milk
6 T. butter, softened and divided
2 eggs
1 c. sugar

1-1/2 c. biscuit baking mix,
   divided
1/2 c. pecans, chopped
1/3 c. brown sugar, packed
Garnish: whipped cream or
   vanilla ice cream

Mix the persimmons and spices and place in a greased 8"x8" pan. Beat
milk, 2 tablespoons butter, eggs, sugar and 1/2 cup biscuit baking mix
until smooth; about 15 seconds in the blender or one minute with a
hand mixer. Pour over persimmons and spices. Mix together
remaining biscuit baking mix, pecans, brown sugar and remaining
butter. Stir until crumbly and sprinkle over fruit. Bake at 325 degrees
for one hour or until a knife inserted in the center comes out clean.
Cool and serve with whipped cream or vanilla ice cream.

*You can still find vintage
enamel lids at tag or yard
sales. Hang one on your
kitchen wall then slip a
homespun dishcloth through
the lid handle.*

Mango Cobbler

Paula Chase
Aurora, CO

This cobbler is so refreshing!

2 c. mangoes, sliced
1-1/4 c. sugar, divided
1 c. all-purpose flour
1 T. baking powder
1/2 t. salt

4-oz. can evaporated milk
1 egg, beaten
1 stick butter
cinnamon to taste

Place mangoes in a medium bowl, cover with water and sprinkle with 1/4 cup of sugar; set aside. Mix dry ingredients together, add milk and egg and mix into a smooth batter. Melt butter in an 8"x8" baking pan. Pour batter over butter; add fruit, don't drain, and sprinkle with cinnamon. Bake at 350 degrees for 40 to 45 minutes. Top should be lightly golden and center should be firm. If you're unable to find fresh mangoes, you can substitute a 16-oz. jar of mangoes found in the produce section. Measure out 2 cups of fruit and add enough of the juice in the jar to barely cover the fruit. Omit the water and cut the amount of sugar listed above in half.

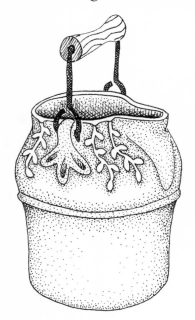

The heart of the giver makes the gift dear and precious; as among ourselves we say; "It comes from the hand we love," and look not so much at the gift as at the heart.

-Martin Luther

Tropical Pineapple Pudding

Teresa Sullivan
Westerville, OH

I like to serve this as a side whenever I make ham for dinner.

1/2 c. margarine, melted
5 white bread slices, cubed
3 eggs, beaten
3 T. all-purpose flour

1/2 t. salt
3/4 c. sugar
20-oz. can crushed pineapple,
   undrained

Place margarine in a large skillet, add bread cubes and sauté until golden; set aside. Place eggs in a large bowl, add flour, salt, sugar and pineapple; mix well. Pour mixture into 1-1/2 quart casserole dish. Add bread cubes, pushing bread down into pineapple mixture. Bake at 350 degrees for 35 to 40 minutes.

He is the very pineapple of politeness.

-Richard Sheridan

Gooseberry Crunch

Ronald Smith
Washington, IN

A very good dessert; I hope you like it!

1 c. all-purpose flour
3/4 c. long-cooking oatmeal
1 c. brown sugar, packed
1/2 c. butter, softened
1 t. cinnamon
1 c. sugar

2 T. cornstarch
1 c. water
1 t. vanilla extract
3 to 4 c. gooseberries
Garnish: whipped cream

Mix together flour, oatmeal, brown sugar, butter and cinnamon until crumbly. Press half of crumbs into a 9"x9" greased pan. In saucepan, combine sugar, cornstarch, water and vanilla. Bring to a boil, add fruit and cook until clear and thick. Pour over crumb mixture and top with remaining crumbs. Bake in a 350 degree oven for 45 minutes or until browned. Cut in squares, serve warm with whipped cream.

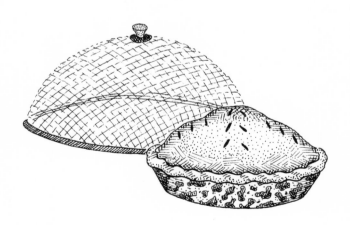

Man's best support is a very dear friend.

-Cicero

Chestnut Farm Apple Crisp

Beth Haney
Edwards, IL

*Add a scoop of vanilla ice cream drizzled with
warm caramel sauce!*

1 stick butter, melted
1 c. brown sugar, packed
1/2 c. apple cider
1/2 c. all-purpose flour
1/4 t. salt
1/2 t. baking powder
1 t. cinnamon

1/4 t. mace
1 c. long-cooking oatmeal
1/2 c. wheat germ
1/2 c. pecans, chopped
4 c. apples, peeled, cored and
    diced

To melted butter, add brown sugar; stir by hand until well blended. Stir in the cider, flour, salt, baking powder, cinnamon and mace; blend well. Add the oatmeal, wheat germ and pecans; stir until blended. Gently fold in the apples. Spread in a greased 9"x9" baking pan. Bake at 350 degrees for 30 minutes or until the top is browned and looks crisp. Makes 8 to 12 servings.

*Tell someone they're the
apple of your eye!
Paint a wooden box red then
paint on a cheerful greeting
or stencil apples
on the outside. Line with
a bread cloth and fill
with delicious apple crisp
or cobbler!*

Crunchy Oat & Fruit Crisp

Sandi Figura
Decatur, IL

A crunchy, fruit-filled crisp that's tasty warm or cold.

1 c. quick-cooking oatmeal
3/4 c. brown sugar, packed and divided
5 T. all-purpose flour, divided
1/3 c. margarine, melted
1 c. blueberries

1 c. cherries
4 apples, peeled, cored and thickly sliced
1/4 c. orange juice concentrate
1 T. cinnamon

Combine oatmeal, 1/2 cup brown sugar, 2 tablespoons flour and margarine together; set aside. In a large bowl, combine fruit and remaining ingredients. Stir until fruit is evenly coated. Spoon filling into an 8"x8" dish. Sprinkle topping over the fruit mixture. Bake at 350 degrees for 30 to 35 minutes or until apples are tender and the topping is golden brown.

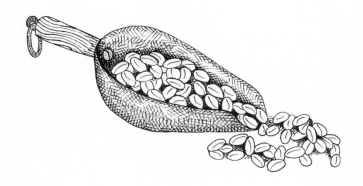

Go oft to the house of thy friend,
for weeds choke the unused path.

-Ralph Waldo Emerson

Friendship Fruit Crumble

Nikkole Kozlowski
Columbus, OH

The secret to this crumble is the tapioca!

10-1/2 oz. can apricot halves,
    drained
16 oz. blueberries
1/3 c. sugar
1 T. lemon juice
1 T. quick-cooking tapioca
1/2 t. cinnamon
1/2 c. brown sugar, packed

1/4 c. all-purpose flour
1/4 c. long-cooking oatmeal
1/2 t. cinnamon
1/4 t. nutmeg
1/2 stick butter, chilled and cut
    into pieces
1/2 c. walnuts, chopped
Garnish: whipped cream

Blend together apricot halves, blueberries, sugar, lemon juice, tapioca
and cinnamon and divide between 4, one-cup custard cups.
Thoroughly mix brown sugar, flour, oatmeal, cinnamon and nutmeg;
cut in butter until mixture resembles coarse crumbs. Fold in nuts and
sprinkle over filling in custard cups. Place custard cups on a cookie
sheet and bake at 375 degrees for 25 minutes. Cool slightly and
garnish with a dollop of whipped cream before serving.

*Thank a friend by sharing this
delicious Friendship Fruit
Crumble. Set the custard cups
in a heart-shaped box and
attach a gift tag that says
"Thanks from the
bottom of my heart."*

Apple Brown Betty

Terri Thompson
Middletown, CT

One of those time-tested recipes we all remember from childhood.

6 to 8 apples, peeled, cored and
    chopped
1 c. sugar
1 c. all-purpose flour
1 t. baking powder

1 t. salt
1 egg, beaten
2 T. butter, melted
cinnamon to taste

Place apples in 9"x9" pie pan; set aside. Mix all dry ingredients together, add egg and pat on top of apples. Drizzle butter over top to completely cover mixture; sprinkle with cinnamon. Bake in a 350 degree oven for 45 minutes.

The first Sunday in August is Friendship Day,
the perfect time for a get-together! Spread blankets on
the ground, set up lots of chairs, fill the picnic table
with goodies and enjoy a day of feasting and fun!

All-Star Cobbler

Coli Harrington
Delaware, OH

*Serve this star-topped dessert on Independence Day with
some homemade, hand-cranked ice cream!*

1-1/4 c. all-purpose flour
1/2 t. salt
1/2 c. shortening, chilled and cut
    into pieces
5 to 6 T. ice water
10-oz. pkg. frozen raspberries,
    thawed, juice reserved

1/4 c. sugar
2 t. cornstarch
1/2 t. cinnamon
1/4 t. nutmeg
2 apples, peeled, cored and
    sliced

Sift together flour and salt; cut in shortening until mixture is crumbly.
Add ice water, one tablespoon at a time, until dough comes together.
Wrap dough in plastic wrap and chill one hour. Add reserved raspberry
juice to a one-cup measuring cup, and add enough water to equal one
cup liquid. Combine sugar, cornstarch, cinnamon and nutmeg in a
saucepan; blend in raspberry liquid. Bring to a boil over medium heat,
stirring constantly, until mixture thickens. Remove from heat and stir
in raspberries and apples. Pour cobbler filling into a 2-quart baking
dish; set aside. Remove dough from refrigerator and roll out to
1/4-inch thickness; cut with a star-shaped cookie cutter. Place stars
over raspberry and apple filling, overlapping if
desired. Bake at 375 degrees for 25
to 30 minutes.

*Change cookie cutter
shapes to go with the
seasons...leaves, flowers,
hearts or snowflakes would
all add a special touch!*

Buttery Blueberry Cobbler

Debra Thornton
DeMotte, IN

Depending on what time of year it is, I've used fresh
peaches and blackberries in this cobbler, too.

1/2 c. butter
1 c. all-purpose flour
1-1/4 c. sugar, divided
1 t. baking powder

1/2 c. milk
2 c. blueberries
1 T. lemon juice

Melt butter in an 8"x8" baking pan. Stir flour, one cup of sugar and baking powder together. Add milk and stir until batter is smooth. Pour evenly over butter; do not stir. Mix berries, lemon juice and remaining sugar in saucepan. Bring to a boil and pour evenly over butter and batter; do not stir. Bake at 350 degrees for 45 minutes.

A handed-down collection of vintage kitchen utensils will bring an old-fashioned charm to your kitchen. Arrange an assortment of graters, sifters, whisks, muffin tins, sugar shakers, butter molds and paddles in baskets, bowls or on shelves.

Grandma's Easy Peach Cobbler

Rene Ray
Delaware, OH

*I know I can always count on this recipe;
it's rich, but oh, so good!*

1 c. all-purpose flour
1 c. sugar
2 t. baking powder
1/2 c. milk

1 stick margarine, melted
29-oz. can sliced peaches with
   juice, divided

Combine flour, sugar and baking powder; mix well. Blend milk into flour mixture until moistened. Add margarine, 3/4 of the peaches and 2/3 of the juice; mix. Spread into 2-quart casserole. Pour remaining peaches and juice over batter; do not stir. Bake at 350 degrees for about 30 minutes.

*A friendship can weather most things and thrive
in thin soil; but it needs a little mulch of letters
and phone calls and small, silly presents every so often.*

-Pam Brown

French Apple Bread Pudding

Bonnie Stanley
Clintwood, VA

Topped with whipped cream, this is terrific!

3 eggs, beaten
12-oz. can sweetened
    condensed milk
3 apples, peeled, cored and
    chopped
1-3/4 c. hot water

1/4 c. butter, melted
1 t. cinnamon
1 t. vanilla extract
4 c. French bread, cubed
1/2 c. raisins
Garnish: whipped cream

In a large bowl, combine eggs, milk, apples, water, butter, cinnamon and vanilla. Stir in bread and raisins, completely moistening bread. Turn into greased 9"x9" pan. Bake at 350 degrees one hour. Garnish with whipped cream.

Put all your eggs in one basket and... watch that basket!

-Mark Twain

Turnovers, Tarts & Dumplings

Mom's Strudel

Melody Faisetty
Whitehall, PA

As a child growing up in the small town of Coplay, Pennsylvania, I remember my mom as a good cook, but also a fantastic baker. It seemed like she'd bake a different cake nearly every day. This nut roll was one of our favorites. She called it "strudel" and it tastes great with a cup of tea.

2 sticks butter
3 eggs, separated and divided
3 c. all-purpose flour
1 c. plus 1 T. sugar, divided

1 pkg. cake yeast
1/2 c. warm milk
7 to 8 oz. walnuts, crushed
1 t. vanilla extract

Mix butter and yolks; add flour. Dissolve one tablespoon sugar and yeast in warm milk and add to the flour mixture. Divide dough into 4 balls. Chill overnight. In small bowl, beat egg whites and combine remaining ingredients; set aside. Roll each dough ball into a rectangle and spread with 1/4 of the filling; roll up jelly roll-style. Bake at 350 degrees on greased cookie sheet until golden. Makes 4 nut rolls.

A good neighbor, like an apron, is comfortable, protecting and always appreciated a lot.

-Claudia Rohling

Blackberry Turnovers

Joshua Logan
Corpus Christi, TX

These are a summer tradition at our house. We always get together as a family to go berry picking; usually eating more berries than we bring home!

1-3/4 c. all-purpose flour
1/4 c. plus 1 T. sugar, divided
1/2 t. salt
2/3 c. shortening, chilled and cut into pieces
2 T. butter, chilled

3 T. water, divided
2 t. cornstarch
16-oz. pkg. frozen blackberries, thawed
3/4 t. cinnamon

Sift together flour, 1/4 cup sugar and salt; cut in shortening and butter until mixture forms coarse crumbs. Stir in 2 tablespoons water, one tablespoon at a time, until a soft dough forms. Wrap in plastic and refrigerate one hour. Dissolve cornstarch in remaining water; set aside. Combine blackberries, remaining sugar and cinnamon in a saucepan, stirring constantly, until mixture boils. Stir in cornstarch mixture until filling begins to thicken. Remove from heat and cool. On a lightly floured surface, roll out dough to 1/8-inch thickness and cut out six, 6-inch circles. Divide filling equally and spoon into the center of each circle. Fold dough over filling and press edges to seal. Place turnovers on an oiled cookie sheet and bake at 400 degrees for 30 minutes. Place on a wire rack to cool completely.

Do you have a collection of old buttons? Use a glue gun to easily attach some of the prettiest ones to a picture frame, then slip one of Grandma's handwritten recipe cards inside the frame... a wonderful keepsake.

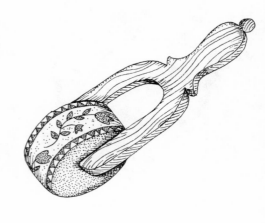

Lemon-Raisin Tarts

Sylvia Mathews
Vancouver, WA

I remember Mama always making these for Dad's birthday and for Christmas. Now I carry on the tradition for my son who gets these melt-in-your-mouth tarts for his birthday and on Christmas.

1/4 lb. butter
2/3 c. sugar
2 eggs
3/4 c. raisins

1/4 c. lemon juice
zest of one lemon
2 9-inch refrigerated pie crusts

Mix butter and sugar; add eggs. Stir in raisins, lemon juice and lemon zest. Let pie crust set at room temperature for 15 minutes, then line muffin tins with pie crusts. Fill each cup 2/3 full with raisin mixture. Bake in a 350 degree oven for 15 to 20 minutes; watch closely. Let cool before you remove muffins from tin.

Why not host a doll party for your daughter and her friends? Spread blankets under shady trees and serve lemonade, doll-size sandwiches and mini tarts. After lunch, the girls and their dolls, can spend the afternoon playing "make believe."

Pecan Tarts

Frankie Stanley
Columbia, IL

My mother is a fabulous cook and is known for her trademark goodies; these pecan tarts! When we had bake sales in high school, Mother always made these. Although they never actually made it to the table...the teachers were the first to buy them!

3-oz. pkg. cream cheese,
    softened
1 stick margarine
1 c. all-purpose flour
1 egg

3/4 c. brown sugar, packed
1/2 t. salt
1 t. vanilla extract
3/4 c. pecans, chopped

Prepare dough by mixing cream cheese, margarine and flour together; chill for one hour. In a large bowl, blend egg, brown sugar and salt; mix well. Blend in vanilla and pecans. Roll dough into 24 balls. Press into tart shells and form into cups. Fill with pecan mixture and bake for 30 minutes at 325 degrees. Cool slightly and remove from pans.

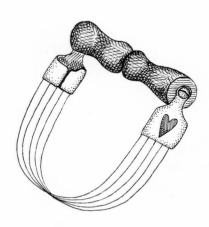

I never get any home cooking...all I see is the fancy stuff.

-Prince Phillip

Apple & Cheddar Dumplings

Beth Kramer
Port Saint Lucie, FL

These are best served still warm with cream poured on top.

8 9-inch refrigerated pie crusts
1/4 c. Cheddar cheese, grated
12 apples, peeled and cored
1/2 c. mincemeat
1-1/2 sticks butter, divided

3/4 c. sugar, divided
1/4 c. brown sugar, packed
1/4 c. whipping cream
zest of 1/2 a lemon

Remove refrigerated pie crusts from packages. Let sit at room temperature for 15 minutes, then cut into twelve, 6"x6" squares. Spoon one teaspoon Cheddar cheese in the center of each square, top with an apple. Fill the center of each apple with 2 teaspoons of mincemeat, a tablespoon butter and one tablespoon sugar. Bring opposite corners of dough together over the apple; pinch together. Blend together brown sugar, cream and lemon zest; brush over dumplings. Bake at 400 degrees for 35 to 45 minutes, or until golden brown.

A trip to the apple orchard will give you plenty of crisp, crunchy apples to share with friends! Write out your favorite recipe for apple dumplings or crisp and give it along with a basket of apples or jar of homemade apple pie filling.

Turnovers, Tarts & Dumplings

Rhubarb Strudel

Tonya Sheppard
Galveston, TX

Sweet and tart...delicious!

4 c. rhubarb, chopped
1 c. sugar
2 T. quick-cooking tapioca
1 t. lemon zest

6 sheets phyllo pastry
1/2 c. butter, melted and divided
1/3 c. bread crumbs, divided

Toss rhubarb with sugar, tapioca and lemon zest; set aside. Lay one sheet of phyllo on damp towel, brush with butter and sprinkle with bread crumbs. Layer remaining phyllo, brushing each sheet with butter and sprinkling with bread crumbs. Spoon rhubarb mixture on the pastry, leaving a 2-inch border around the edges. Carefully roll the phyllo over rhubarb filling jelly roll-style, tucking in the edges as you roll. Place strudel, seam-side down, on an oiled cookie sheet. Brush with remaining melted butter and cut several diagonal slits in the top. Bake at 400 degrees for 30 to 35 minutes or until golden.

If you're visiting a new mom, take along a home-baked dessert. Paint a bread basket a favorite color, line with a paper doily and set your strudel inside. She'll love the chance to visit and enjoy your treat!

Triple Berry Tart

Gail Prather
Bethel, MN

Three of my favorite summertime berries are in this tart;
our family thinks it's the best!

1 c. all-purpose flour
1/4 c. plus 2 T. sugar, divided
1/4 t. salt
1/2 c. butter, sliced
2 T. walnuts, finely chopped
1-3/4 c. plus 2 T. sour cream,
    divided
1/4 oz. pkg. unflavored gelatin
5 T. water
1/2 c. blueberries

1/3 c. blackberries
1/3 c. raspberries
1 c. plain yogurt
1/2 t. vanilla extract
1/4 c. plus 2 T. orange juice
2 T. brown sugar, packed
1 to 2 t. orange zest
Garnish: fresh berries and
    mint leaves

In a large bowl, combine flour, 2 tablespoons sugar and salt; cut in
butter until crumbly. Stir in walnuts and 2 tablespoons sour cream,
one tablespoon at a time, until dough forms a ball. Flatten ball slightly;
wrap in plastic wrap. Refrigerate about 30 minutes. On a lightly
floured surface, roll out dough into 12-inch circle and place in a 9" tart
pan with removable bottom. Bake at 350 degrees for 18 to 22 minutes
or until lightly browned; set aside. In one-quart saucepan, combine
gelatin and water. Cook over medium heat, stirring constantly, until
gelatin is completely dissolved, about 2 to 3 minutes. Remove from
heat. In 5-cup blender, combine blueberries, blackberries and
raspberries. Cover; blend at high speed for one minute or until puréed.
Place in medium bowl. Stir in 1/4 cup sugar, yogurt, 3/4 cup sour
cream and vanilla. With wire whisk, stir in gelatin mixture and pour
filling into crust. Refrigerate, covered, for 3 hours. To prepare sauce,
stir together orange juice and brown sugar. Whisk in one cup sour
cream and orange zest. Cover and refrigerate 30 minutes. Spoon
sauce over individual servings and garnish with fresh berries and
mint leaves.

Glazed Nectarine Dumplings

Melanie Lowe
Dover, DE

The tart lemon glaze makes these dumplings special!

1-1/2 c. all-purpose flour
1/4 t. salt
7 T. butter, chilled, cut into
  pieces
1 egg, beaten
1 T. butter, softened
1 T. sugar

1 T. almonds, ground
3 t. lemon juice, divided
4 nectarines, peeled and pitted
1 c. whipping cream
2 T. powdered sugar
2 t. lemon zest

Sift together flour and salt; use a pastry blender and cut in chilled butter. Add egg, stirring until a soft dough forms. Refrigerate dough for 30 minutes while preparing filling. Mix together softened butter, sugar, almonds and one teaspoon lemon juice. Spoon mixture into center of each nectarine. Remove dough from refrigerator and roll in a 12-inch square; cut square in four 6-inch squares. Place a nectarine in the center of each square and wrap dough around nectarine; pinch to seal. Place dumplings on an oiled baking sheet. Bake dumplings at 400 degrees for 20 minutes or until golden. Blend together cream, powdered sugar, remaining lemon juice and lemon zest. Simmer until thick, about 5 minutes. Spoon sauce over warm dumplings.

...this moment I was writing with one hand and with the other holding to my mouth a nectarine...how fine!

-John Keats

Angel Strudel

Jo Baker
Litchfield, IL

At our house, and at my grandmother's farm home, we kept busy from morning until night. We rarely left our community, which created an opportunity for neighbors to get together for dancing at the hall and sampling each other's delicacies. We generously traded recipes and this is one I've never seen printed.

1 c. butter
2 c. all-purpose flour
3 egg yolks
2 T. vinegar
1/4 c. water

1 c. walnuts, ground
1 c. maraschino cherries, chopped
18-1/4 oz. box angel food cake mix

Cut butter into flour; set aside. Mix egg yolks, vinegar and water; add to flour mixture. Divide dough into 4 rolls, cover and refrigerate overnight. When ready to prepare strudel, roll out one portion of dough, very thin, into a rectangle. Prepare filling by combining walnuts, cherries and cake mix; divide into 4 equal parts. Spread one quarter of the filling on rolled dough and roll up jelly roll-style. Repeat with remaining 3 portions of dough and filling. Bake each strudel at 325 degrees for 25 minutes.

Great cooking is the source of true happiness.

-Escoffier

New England Cinnamon Tart

Regina Vining
Warwick, RI

Peaches wrapped in a cinnamon crust...yummy!

2-1/2 c. all-purpose flour
1-1/4 c. sugar, divided
1/4 t. baking powder
2 T. cinnamon
1 stick butter, chilled and cut
    into pieces

1/2 c. cold water, divided
1 c. apricot jam
8 to 10 peaches, peeled, pitted
    and sliced

Sift together flour, 3/4 cup sugar, baking powder and cinnamon;
cut in butter. Add cold water, one tablespoon at a time, to flour
mixture, forming a soft dough. On a lightly floured surface, roll dough
out to a 10-inch circle; chill about 30 minutes. Place dough in a 9" pie
pan and bake at 350 degrees for 15 to 20 minutes, or until golden.
To prepare apricot glaze, blend together jam, remaining sugar and
water in a saucepan. Bring to a boil, reduce heat and simmer until
clear. Arrange peaches in baked tart crust. Lightly brush peaches with
glaze and serve.

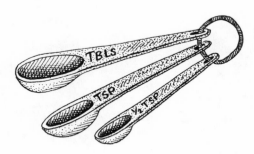

Cover the outside of a 10-inch round box with beautiful
harvest-colored fabric; it's easy to attach with spray adhesive.
Set your tart inside, close the box and add a gift tag that
reads "Gobble Up!" Great for a Thanksgiving dinner!

Chess Tarts

Liz Plotnick
Gooseberry Patch

These tiny tarts are great for a holiday buffet table.

4 eggs
2 c. brown sugar, packed
2 T. all-purpose flour
6 T. unsalted butter, melted
1 T. vinegar

1/4 c. whipping cream
1 t. lemon zest
10 tart shells, unbaked
10 nut halves

Beat together eggs, brown sugar, flour, butter, vinegar, cream and lemon zest. Pour into tart shells; top each with a nut half. Bake at 375 degrees for 10 minutes. Makes 10 tarts.

Wrap several tiny tarts in wax paper tied with raffia then nestle them in something small...an antique sifter, handmade mitten, old-fashioned sugar sack or vintage salt crock. The thoughtful container will be a reminder of friendship long after the tarts are gone.

Creamy Raisin Strudel

Claire Bertram
Lexington, KY

*If you're short on time, just make the raisin filling
the day before, wrap well and chill.*

1-1/2 c. ricotta cheese
8-oz. pkg. cream cheese,
  softened
1/2 c. sugar
1 egg

1/2 c. raisins
1 T. lemon zest
8 sheets phyllo dough
3 T. butter, melted and divided
1 T. powdered sugar

Beat together ricotta, cream cheese, sugar and egg until well blended.
Fold in raisins and lemon zest; set aside. Unfold phyllo sheets and
layer 4 sheets on plastic wrap. Brush the top sheet with one
tablespoon butter, then spoon on half the raisin filling along the short
side of the top phyllo sheet. Beginning with the short side, roll all
4 sheets of phyllo, jelly roll-style; press edges to seal. Place strudel,
seam-side down on an oiled cookie sheet. Brush strudel with
1/2 tablespoon of butter and score the top with a sharp knife. Layer
remaining 4 sheets of phyllo and repeat to make a second strudel.
Bake strudels at 400 degrees until golden, 20 to 25 minutes. Cool
completely and sprinkle with powdered sugar.

*The way to a man's
heart is through
his stomach!*

-Sarah Payson Parton

Good but other recipes @ better in my cookbook

Crumbly Rhubarb Tart

Connie Bryant
Topeka, KS

We love this treat warm from the oven! It's tart, so you can substitute raspberries if you'd prefer, but this is really good!

1-1/2 c. all-purpose flour, divided
1 t. baking powder
3 T. powdered sugar
2/3 c. butter, divided

1 egg, beaten
4 t. milk
3 c. rhubarb, diced
3-oz. pkg. strawberry gelatin
3/4 1 c. sugar

Sift together one cup flour, baking powder and powdered sugar; cut in 1/3 cup butter. Stir in egg and milk to form a soft dough and pat into an oiled 11"x7" baking pan. Spoon rhubarb on crust; sprinkle dry gelatin over rhubarb. Combine remaining flour, butter and sugar until crumbly; add to top of rhubarb filling. Bake at 350 degrees for 45 to 50 minutes; cool completely.

Set aside a sunny afternoon to host a pie party for friends and neighbors! Set several tables under shady trees and layer them with quilts or old-fashioned ticking. Ask friends to bring their favorite pie, and the recipe, to share and you provide the coffee, milk, plates, cups and forks.

Peach Pocket Dumplings

Dale Duncan
Waterloo, IA

We like these because the peaches are coated with a
crunchy brown sugar topping; they're delicious!

2 c. all-purpose flour
1 t. salt
2/3 c. shortening, chilled and
    cut into pieces
1/4 c. ice water
3/4 stick butter, softened

6 T. sugar
2 T. walnuts, chopped
1-1/2 t. cinnamon
6 peaches, peeled and pitted
1 c. brown sugar, packed
1/2 c. plus 6 T. water, divided

Sift together flour and salt; cut in shortening using a pastry blender or
2 knives. Add ice water, one tablespoon at a time, until mixture forms
a soft dough; chill 30 minutes. Combine butter, sugar, nuts and
cinnamon until well blended; spoon equal amounts into center of
peaches. Roll dough to 1/8-inch thick and cut into six 6-inch squares.
Place one peach in the center of each dough square; brush dough
edges with one tablespoon water and wrap around peach; pinch edges
to seal. Place dumplings in a greased 13"x9" baking dish and bake at
400 degrees for 10 minutes. Blend together brown sugar and
remaining water; bring to a boil and simmer 5 minutes. Reduce oven
to 350 degrees, spoon brown sugar syrup over dumplings. Bake until
golden, about 40 minutes longer.

BLESS THIS KITCHEN

On days when warmth is
the most important
need of the human heart,
the kitchen is the place
you can find it...

-E.B. White

Mom's Apple Dumplings

Jill Valentine
Jackson, TN

There's nothing like Mom's dumplings. They remind me of apple picking with the family. We'd always eat a few apples on the way home, then beg Mom to make these dumplings for dessert!

2 c. all-purpose flour
1 t. salt
2/3 c. shortening, chilled and
    cut into pieces
1/4 to 1/2 c. ice water
3-1/2 T. butter, softened
1/3 c. brown sugar, packed
1 t. cinnamon
3/4 t. allspice

1/2 t. nutmeg
3-1/2 T. orange marmalade
1-1/2 T. raisins
1/8 t. cloves
8 med. apples, peeled and cored
1-1/2 c. sugar
1-1/2 c. plus 8 T. water, divided
3 T. orange juice

Blend together flour and salt; cut in shortening to form coarse crumbs. Add ice water to flour, one tablespoon at a time, until a dough forms; chill 30 minutes. Combine butter, brown sugar, cinnamon, allspice and nutmeg; set aside. In separate bowl, blend together marmalade, raisins and cloves. On a lightly floured surface, roll dough out 1/8 to 1/4-inch thickness and cut into eight 6-inch circles. Moisten edges of each dough circle with one tablespoon water and set apple in the center. Fill each apple with marmalade mixture and spread butter mixture over outside of apples. Wrap dough around apples, pinching dough to seal edges. Place dumplings in a greased 13"x9" baking pan. Bake dumplings at 375 degrees for 30 minutes or until pastry is golden. Mix together sugar, 1-1/2 cups water and orange juice over medium heat, stirring constantly, until sugar dissolves. Pour over dumplings and continue to bake another 15 minutes.

If you have extra dough, roll it out and cut out a variety of leaf shapes. Brush one side with milk and gently attach the "leaves" to the top of your apple dumpling before baking!

Cherry Turnovers

Lynda Robson
Boston, MA

*These are so quick and easy, but taste like you spent
hours in the kitchen making them!*

17-1/4 oz. pkg. frozen puff
  pastry, thawed
21-oz. can cherry pie filling,
  drained

1 c. powdered sugar
2 T. water

Separate puff pastry sheets and cut each into 4 squares. Divide pie
filling equally among each square, brush the pastry edges with
water and fold in half diagonally. Seal and crimp edges with a fork
and bake on an ungreased baking sheet at 400 degrees for 15 to
18 minutes or until puffed and golden. Let turnovers slightly cool.
Blend together powdered sugar and 2 tablespoons water, drizzle
over the warm turnovers.

Life is just a bowl of cherries!

-Anonymous

Rustic Pear Tart

Melody Taynor
Everett, WA

Simple to make, this tart can make one large or many bite-size tarts!

1 c. plus 2 T. all-purpose flour, divided
1/4 c. plus 1 T. plus 1 t. sugar, divided
1/4 t. baking powder
1/4 t. salt
4 T. plus 1 t. unsalted butter, chilled, cut into pieces and divided

3 T. sour cream
1-1/2 lbs. pears, peeled, cored and sliced
1 T. lemon juice
1/2 t. vanilla extract
2 t. powdered sugar

Sift together one cup flour, one teaspoon sugar, baking powder and salt; cut in 4 tablespoons butter until mixture resembles coarse meal. Stir in sour cream and stir with a fork until the mixture is very crumbly and fine. Cover dough and chill 30 minutes. Combine pears and lemon juice, 1/4 cup sugar and vanilla; toss to coat. On a lightly floured surface, roll dough to a 14-inch circle. Place circle on an ungreased baking sheet. Mix together remaining flour and one tablespoon sugar and sprinkle evenly over the dough. Lay pear slices over the sugar mixture, moisten dough edges with water and fold dough in 2 inches over the pears. Dot the pears with the butter and bake at 400 degrees for 40 minutes, or until the crust is golden. Cool 15 minutes and dust with powdered sugar.

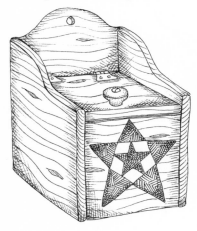

Who ran to help me when I fell,
and would some pretty story tell,
or kiss the place to make it well?
My mother.

-Ann Taylor

Homemade Jam Crescents

Regina Vining
Warwick, RI

I've used blackberry, boysenberry and strawberry jam in these crescents and they've all tasted great!

1/4 c. sugar
1 t. cardamom
1/2 t. salt
2 c. all-purpose flour
2 t. baking powder

1 stick margarine, chilled and
   cut into pieces
1 T. egg, beaten
1/4 c. milk
1/2 c. red raspberry jam

Sift together sugar, cardamom, salt, flour and baking powder; cut in margarine until mixture resembles coarse crumbs. Add egg and milk; blend until a soft dough forms. On a lightly floured surface, roll dough into a 20"x8" rectangle. Cut down the middle of the pastry to make two 20-inch long strips. Cut each strip into 5 equal squares, then cut each square on the diagonal; you'll have 20 triangles. Spoon a teaspoon of jam onto each triangle and roll into a crescent shape. Place several crescents on a lightly oiled baking sheet and bake at 450 degrees for 8 to 10 minutes or until golden.

A plate of freshly-baked crescents and a jar of homemade jam would be a perfect hostess gift. Don't forget to share your recipes for the the jam and crescents!

Blueberry & Peach Turnovers

Wendy Jacobs
Idaho Falls, ID

I love the taste of blueberries and peaches; they just seem to go together so well! This recipe was shared by a dear friend.

1-1/4 c. blueberries
1 peach, peeled, pitted and
　chopped
1-1/4 c. sugar

1/8 t. nutmeg
6 sheets frozen phyllo pastry,
　thawed
1/4 c. butter, melted

Spoon blueberries and peach into a bowl. Sprinkle on sugar and nutmeg, stir and set aside for 15 minutes. Cut each phyllo sheet lengthwise into four 3-1/2" wide strips; lightly brush with melted butter. Stack 2 phyllo strips, one on top of the other. Spoon one table-spoon blueberry-peach mixture onto one end of each stack; fold the left bottom corner over mixture, forming a triangle. Keep folding back and forth, as if you were folding a flag. Repeat with remaining ingredients. Place the turnovers, seam-side down on an ungreased baking sheet. Lightly brush with butter and bake at 400 degrees for 15 minutes. Makes 12 turnovers.

*Make a keepsake box
for a close friend or sister.
Cover the lid of a round Shaker box
with vintage buttons, yo-yo's or charms.
An old spool in the middle would
make a perfect knob for the box.
Add a small frame with a favorite
photograph of the two of you.*

Brown Sugar & Raisin Tarts

Virginia Watson
Scranton, PA

An old family recipe, handed down for many years…it's one of my husband's favorite recipes when he has a sweet tooth!

2 9-inch refrigerated pie crusts
1 c. raisins, finely chopped
1/2 c. walnuts, chopped
1/2 c. brown sugar, packed
3 T. butter, softened

3 T. orange juice
1 egg, beaten
2-1/2 T. half-and-half
Garnish: whipping cream

Using a small round biscuit cutter, cut refrigerated pie crusts into 2-inch rounds and place in a mini muffin pan. Combine raisins, walnuts, brown sugar, butter, orange juice, egg and half-and-half. Spoon mixture equally among tarts. Bake at 425 degrees for 20 minutes or until pastry is lightly golden. Makes one dozen small tarts. Garnish with whipping cream.

The best antiques are old friends.

-Anonymous

Cinnamon-Peach Puffs

Dana Cunningham
Lafayette, LA

You could substitute apples for the peaches if you'd like; I've even used fresh pears in this recipe; they've worked great!

1 sheet frozen puff pastry,
    thawed
7 med. peaches, peeled, pitted
    and thinly sliced
2/3 c. sugar

1/2 stick butter, softened
2 T. lemon juice
1/2 t. cinnamon
1/4 t. salt
1/4 t. nutmeg

On a lightly floured surface, roll pastry to 1/8-inch thickness. Using a sharp knife, cut dough into eight 5-inch squares. Place pastry squares on a lightly oiled baking sheet and freeze for one hour. Blend together peaches, sugar, butter, lemon juice, cinnamon, salt and nutmeg. Spoon peach filling in the center of each pastry square and fold corners of dough toward the middle, don't pinch together. Bake at 375 degrees for 25 to 30 minutes. Cool on wire racks.

Kissing don't last; cookery do!

-George Meredith

Apricot Pockets

Sandy Taranto
North Haledon, NJ

These are my favorite because they melt in your mouth!

1 stick butter
3-oz. pkg. cream cheese
1 c. all-purpose flour

16-oz. can apricot halves,
    drained
1 c. sugar
1/2 c. powdered sugar

Mix together butter, cream cheese and flour; form a ball. Wrap in plastic wrap and refrigerate overnight. Work dough until soft. Roll out on a floured board. Cut dough into twelve 3-inch squares. Take each apricot half, roll in sugar and place into a square. Fold up corners to the center to form a pocket. Bake at 350 degrees for 20 to 25 minutes on parchment-covered cookie sheet until light brown. When cool, sprinkle with powdered sugar. Makes one dozen.

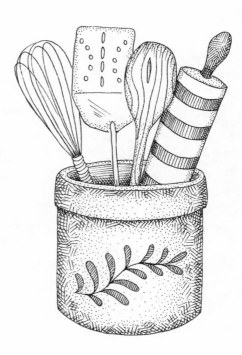

Have the kids paint "I love you" or "#1 Mom!" on a wooden tray. Have little ones add their painted handprints, then Dad can write on their names and ages. Great for Mom's breakfast in bed!

Strawberry-Rhubarb Pastries

Samantha Starks
Madison, WI

*This recipe combines my two favorite flavors! It's like eating a
strawberry-rhubarb pie, but the puff pastry is so flaky!*

1 sheet frozen puff pastry,
   thawed

1 c. rhubarb, chopped
1/2 c. strawberry jam

On a lightly floured surface, cut puff pastry into six 5"x3" pieces, then
roll out pastry into 6-inch squares. Blend together rhubarb and jam
and spoon evenly into the center of each pastry square. Moisten the
edges of the pastry with water, and pull the corners to the center,
pinching to seal. Place on an ungreased baking sheet and bake at
425 degrees for 5 minutes; reduce heat to 350 degrees and bake
20 minutes longer. Cool on a wire rack.

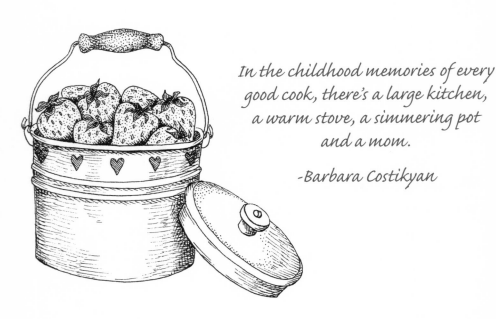

*In the childhood memories of every
good cook, there's a large kitchen,
a warm stove, a simmering pot
and a mom.*

-Barbara Costikyan

Country-Style Pear Dumplings

Rita Morgan
Pueblo, CO

The caramel sauce makes these dumplings extra special!

2 c. all-purpose flour
2-1/2 t. baking powder
1 t. salt
2/3 c. shortening, chilled and
    cut into pieces
1/2 c. milk

1 c. pineapple juice
1/2 c. water
1/2 c. brown sugar, packed
1/2 stick butter
4 pears, peeled and cored
2-1/2 T. sugar

Thoroughly blend flour, baking powder and salt; cut in shortening. Stir in milk, one tablespoon at a time, until mixture forms a soft dough. Wrap in plastic and chill 30 minutes. Blend together pineapple juice, water, brown sugar and butter in a saucepan. Heat over low temperature until butter melts and sugar dissolves. On a lightly floured surface, roll dough to a 13-inch square; cut into four 6-inch squares. Place a pear in the center of each square and brush the dough edges with water. Bring 4 corners of dough together at top and pinch corners together. Place dumplings in an oiled 8"x8" baking dish, sprinkle with sugar and pour sauce over top. Bake at 375 degrees for 45 minutes.

Share your favorite recipe! Place all the dry ingredients in plastic zipping bags then tuck them in a colorful oven mitt. Tie on the recipe and give to a new friend.

Apple Danish

Joy Hayden
Goodland, KS

Enjoy this terrific apple treat...one of our family's favorites!

4 c. plus 2 T. all-purpose flour,
    divided
1/2 t. salt
1-1/2 c. shortening
1/2 to 3/4 c. water
8 to 9 apples, peeled, cored and
    sliced

1-1/2 c. sugar
2 t. cinnamon
1/2 stick margarine
3 c. powdered sugar
1-1/2 t. vanilla extract
7 to 8 t. milk

Blend 4 cups flour and salt; cut in shortening with pastry blender or 2 knives. Add water until pastry forms a ball. Roll out 1/2 of dough and place in greased 16"x11" pan. Arrange apples evenly over dough. Combine sugar, remaining flour and cinnamon; sprinkle over apples. Dot with margarine. Roll out remaining dough and place over top of apples. Fold lower crust over top crust. Do not crimp edges. Bake at 375 degrees for 45 minutes. After the Danish has cooled, combine powdered sugar, vanilla and milk. Mix until smooth and drizzle over the top of the crust.

Give an apple Danish to a favorite teacher...
deliver it with a tiny slate gift tag!

Berry Fold-Ups

Sherry Gordon
Arlington Heights, IL

These are great served with a cup of herbal tea.
The puff pastry is sweet and delicious!

1/4 c. sugar
2 T. cornstarch
2 T. bread crumbs
1-3/4 c. strawberries

1 sheet frozen puff pastry,
  thawed
1 egg
1 T. water
powdered sugar

Combine sugar, cornstarch and bread crumbs; sprinkle over strawberries and toss well. On a lightly floured surface, cut pastry into 9 equal
pieces, then roll each piece into a 6-inch square. Spoon 3 tablespoons
of strawberry mixture into the center of each square; set aside. Mix
together egg and water and brush along edges of pastry. Bring corners
to center and cover filling; pinch to seal. Place pastries on an ungreased
baking sheet and bake at 400 degrees for 10 minutes, reduce heat to
350 degrees and bake 15 to 20 minutes longer. Cool for 5 minutes
then dust with powdered sugar.

Berry fold-ups will be a hit at
the Independence Day celebration
when you bring them in a
star-spangled bag! Use fusible web
to attach patriotic fabric to a brown
paper bag; fold down top to make
a cuff. Fill a plastic zipping bag
with berry fold-ups and tuck inside!

Applesauce Turnovers

Helen Murray
Piketon, OH

These turnovers are so versatile, you can easily substitute your favorite flavor of preserves for the raisin filling.

1-1/2 c. applesauce
1/2 c. raisins
1/2 c. walnuts, chopped
1/2 t. cinnamon

4 9-inch refrigerated pie crusts
6 T. water
6 T. milk
1/4 c. powdered sugar

Mix applesauce, raisins, walnuts and cinnamon together. Using a 4-1/2 inch round biscuit cutter or glass dipped in sugar, cut pie crusts into 10 rounds. Place a tablespoon of filling in the center of each round, moisten edges with water, fold in half, seal with fork tines. Brush with milk and prick steam holes in the top of each. Bake turnovers at 400 degrees for 15 to 20 minutes or until golden. Sprinkle with powdered sugar while warm. Makes 10 turnovers.

Good things baked in the kitchen will keep romance far longer than bright lipstick.

-Marjorie Husted

Golden Delicious Turnovers

Tiffany Brinkley
Broomfield, CO

This couldn't be more old-fashioned; it reminds me of growing up in the country and spending time with my grandmother!

1 c. raisins
1 T. vanilla extract
2 T. water
1 Golden Delicious apple, peeled,
   cored and diced

1/3 c. brown sugar, packed
1/2 t. cinnamon
2 sheets frozen puff pastry,
   thawed
2 eggs, beaten and divided

In microwave-safe bowl, blend together raisins, vanilla and water. Cover with plastic wrap and microwave on high for 45 seconds. Let cool 5 minutes, then blend in apple, brown sugar and cinnamon; stir well. Cut each sheet of pastry into 4 squares and spoon an equal amount of raisin mixture in the center of each square. Brush edges of squares with one egg and fold in half to make triangles; use the tines of a fork to seal edges. Brush tops with remaining egg. Make small slits in top of each turnover and place on a greased baking sheet. Bake at 400 degrees for 15 to 20 minutes or until golden and puffed. Makes 8 turnovers.

Spend an afternoon sharing favorite recipes with a friend. Together you'll have some tasty new dishes to serve your families!

Black Raspberry Packets

Robin Hill
Rochester, NY

You could substitute apple butter for the preserves if you'd like; just add a dash of cinnamon and you've got another great treat!

1 pkg. active dry yeast
1/4 c. warm water
1/2 stick butter
1 c. milk
1/2 c. ricotta cheese
6 T. sugar

1/2 t. salt
4 to 4-1/2 c. all-purpose flour
1/2 c. black raspberry preserves
1/2 t. cornstarch
1 egg, beaten
1/2 c. sugar

Sprinkle yeast in warm water; stir to dissolve and let stand until mixture foams; 5 to 10 minutes. Combine butter and milk in a small saucepan and cook until butter melts; cool to lukewarm. Blend into yeast mixture and set aside for 2 minutes. Stir in ricotta cheese, sugar and salt. Add flour, 1/2 cup at a time, until a dough forms. Knead on a lightly floured surface for 10 minutes. Shape into a ball and place in an oiled bowl, turning to coat all sides. Let rise until double in size, about one hour. Punch down dough and roll out on a lightly floured surface into a 20-inch square, then cut dough into 4-inch squares. Thoroughly combine preserves and cornstarch and spoon in the center of each square. Moisten pastry edges with water, fold dough over to make triangle and pinch to seal. Place packets on a greased baking sheet and let rise 30 minutes. Brush with egg and sprinkle with sugar. Bake at 425 degrees for 10 minutes. Makes 25 packets.

All's well that ends with a good meal.

-Arnold Lobel

Sweet Cherry Triangles

Carrie O'Shea
Marina Del Ray, CA

Yummy...like biting into a mini cherry pie!

1-1/4 c. all-purpose flour
1 t. sugar, divided
1/4 t. salt
1 stick butter, chilled and cut
    into pieces
2 to 3 T. cold water

16-1/2 oz. can pitted, dark
    sweet cherries, drained
1/4 c. cherry preserves
3/4 t. cinnamon, divided
2 eggs, beaten and divided

Mix together flour, 1/2 teaspoon sugar and salt, use a pastry blender or 2 knives to cut in butter. Add water, one tablespoon at a time, until a dough begins to form. Wrap and refrigerate for one hour. Roll dough out to a 12"x8" rectangle; cut into six 4-inch squares. Thoroughly blend cherries, preserves and 1/2 teaspoon cinnamon; spoon equally into the center of each square. Brush one egg along the edges of the dough and fold into a triangle. Use the tines of a fork to seal edges. Brush remaining egg over turnovers; sprinkle with remaining sugar and cinnamon. Bake at 425 degrees for 15 minutes or until golden brown.

If you cross stitch, it's easy
to make a personalized gift for
a friend! On a 5-inch fabric square,
cross stitch something fun,
like "Corrine's Cookies".
Glue batting to a canning jar lid,
top with stitched square,
then glue inside jar ring.
Let dry and fill your jar with goodies!

Caramel-Nut Tart

Lisa Watkins
Gooseberry Patch

To make each slice extra-special, top with a dollop of
whipped cream and chocolate shavings.

3 c. pecans, chopped and
    divided
1/3 c. slivered almonds
3 T. sugar
1/3 c. butter, softened

1 t. vanilla extract
28 caramel squares
1/3 c. half-and-half
3 T. semi-sweet chocolate chips
1 t. oil

Combine 1-1/2 cups pecans, almonds and sugar in a food processor until finely ground, but not pasty; set aside. Blend together butter and vanilla extract; add ground nut mixture. Gently press into the bottom of a 9" tart pan. Bake at 350 degrees for 20 minutes or until golden. Remove to a rack and let cool completely. In a large saucepan over medium heat, combine caramels and half-and-half until mixture is smooth. Spoon over crust; top with remaining pecans. Let caramel cool and set until firm, about 30 minutes. Melt together chocolate chips and oil, stir to blend then drizzle over tart. Serves 12.

Visit antique shops or tag sales and look for small vintage tart tins. You can find them in all shapes... hearts, flowers, fluted circles and rectangles. Use them instead of your large tart pan for perfect bite-size tarts!

Cookies & Brownies

Caramel Brownies

Jody Komarnitzki
Venice, FL

A great after-school treat with a glass of icy cold cider!

7-oz. pkg. caramels
2/3 c. evaporated milk, divided
18-1/4 oz. box German
    chocolate cake mix

2/3 c. butter
1 c. pecans, chopped
12-oz. pkg. chocolate chips

Combine caramels and 1/3 cup evaporated milk in a microwave-safe bowl. Heat, stirring occasionally, until caramels have melted. Combine cake mix with remaining 1/3 cup milk and butter. Press half of cake in a greased and floured 9"x9" pan and bake at 350 degrees for 8 minutes. Remove from oven. Scatter chocolate chips on crust, then drizzle melted caramels over chips. Drop remaining cake mixture by spoonfuls on top of caramels and continue to bake for an additional 18 minutes. Let cool before cutting.

Give a "special delivery" package to a new neighbor or out-of-town visitor! Fill a painted crate with tins of homemade brownies and cookies, a map of the local shops and fun places to visit as well as important phone numbers.

Orange Cookies

Diane Long
Delaware, OH

My husband's great-grandparents immigrated from Switzerland and settled in a small Ohio town. This recipe came with them and was made by his grandmother for many holiday desserts.

2 c. sugar
1 c. shortening
2 eggs
juice and zest of 2 oranges,
    divided
1 c. sour cream

1 T. baking soda
5 c. all-purpose flour
2 T. baking powder
1/8 t. salt
16-oz. pkg. powdered sugar
2 T. butter, melted

Mix sugar, shortening, eggs, juice and zest of one orange and sour cream. Sift together baking soda, flour, baking powder and salt; add to egg mixture. Drop by tablespoonfuls on an ungreased baking sheet. Bake at 350 degrees for 7 to 8 minutes. To make frosting, mix together remaining zest and juice, powdered sugar and butter. Frost cookies when cool.

Come and share my pot of tea,
my home is warm
and my friendship's free.

-Anonymous

Raisin-Spice Cookies

Barbara Daubenmier
Granbury, TX

A good, old-fashioned cookie recipe right from Grandma's cookie jar.

1 c. margarine
1 c. molasses
1 c. buttermilk
2 eggs, beaten
1 c. sugar
4 to 4-1/2 c. all-purpose flour

2 t. baking powder
1 t. baking soda
1 t. ginger
1/2 t. cinnamon
1 c. raisins

Beat together margarine, molasses, buttermilk and eggs. Blend remaining dry ingredients together and stir gradually into the margarine mixture. Drop on ungreased baking sheet and bake for 15 to 20 minutes at 350 degrees. If desired, frost with your favorite icing.

Vintage cookie jars can be found at flea markets or tag sales. Fill them with cookies and a favorite recipe. . .wonderful for a new bride.

Fudgy Oatmeal Bars

Becky Sykes
Gooseberry Patch

I like to tuck these into my daughters' lunchboxes.

2 c. brown sugar, packed
1 c. plus 2 T. margarine,
    softened and divided
2 t. vanilla extract, divided
2 eggs
2-1/2 c. all-purpose flour
1 t. baking soda

1 t. salt, divided
3 c. quick-cooking oatmeal
14-oz. can sweetened condensed
    milk
12-oz. pkg. chocolate chips
1 c. walnuts, chopped

Mix brown sugar, one cup margarine, one teaspoon vanilla and eggs.
Sift together flour, baking soda and 1/2 teaspoon salt; stir in oatmeal
and add to egg mixture. Reserve 1/3 of the oatmeal mixture; press
remaining oatmeal mixture into greased jelly roll pan. Heat
2 tablespoons margarine, condensed milk and chocolate chips over
low heat, stirring constantly until chocolate is melted; remove from
heat. Stir in nuts, remaining vanilla and salt. Spread over oatmeal
mixture in pan. Drop reserved oatmeal mixture by rounded
teaspoonfuls onto chocolate mixture. Bake at 350 degrees for 25 to
30 minutes or until golden brown. Cut into bars while warm.

*A great Mother's Day
gift...have the kids paint an
apron for Mom! They can
paint their hands and gently
press on the fabric, add their
names or even write their
favorite cookie recipe right
on the front!*

Birthday Brownies

Mary Ann Clark
Indian Springs, OH

My children often request this quick and easy
recipe as treats for their birthday.

3/4 c. margarine, softened
1-1/4 c. sugar
1-1/4 c. brown sugar, packed
3 eggs
1 t. vanilla extract

1/2 t. salt
2-1/2 t. baking powder
2-1/4 c. all-purpose flour
12-oz. pkg. chocolate chips

Cream margarine and sugars together until very smooth. Add eggs, vanilla, salt and baking powder. Mix in flour, add chocolate chips and spread in a buttered 13"x9" pan. Bake at 400 degrees for 20 minutes or until toothpick inserted in center comes out clean. Makes 16 large brownies.

Chewy Chocolate Cookies

Margaret Scoresby
Mount Vernon, OH

Add chocolate chips for a richer cookie!

1/2 c. shortening
1-2/3 c. sugar
2 eggs
2 t. vanilla extract
5 T. cocoa

2 c. all-purpose flour
2 t. baking powder
1/2 t. salt
1/3 c. milk
1/2 c. nuts, chopped

Cream shortening and sugar. Add eggs and vanilla; stir in cocoa. Sift together remaining ingredients and add to cocoa mixture alternately with milk. Drop by spoonfuls on ungreased cookie sheet. Bake at 350 degrees for 8 to 10 minutes.

Cherish all your happy moments. . .

-Christopher Morley

Devil's Food Sandwich Cookies

Sheila Gwaltney
Johnson City, TN

A favorite cookie for dunking in milk!

18-1/4 oz. pkg. devil's food cake mix	8-oz. pkg. cream cheese 1/2 c. margarine
3/4 c. shortening	1/2 t. almond extract
2 eggs	16-oz. pkg. powdered sugar

Combine cake mix, shortening and eggs together. Form into small balls and flatten slightly on ungreased cookie sheet. Bake at 350 degrees for 8 to 10 minutes; let cool. In medium bowl, blend cream cheese, margarine and almond extract. Gradually blend in powdered sugar until desired consistency. Beat with a spoon until smooth, refrigerate. When cookies are cool, spread filling between 2 cookies, repeat. Best if kept refrigerated.

Have a fun after-school snack for the kids. Bake their favorite cookies, fill old-fashioned milk bottles with milk and enjoy some time together while you talk about their day at school.

Date-Filled Cookies

Adele Peterman
Austin, TX

A recipe handed down from my grandmother; it's a family favorite!

1-1/3 c. sugar
2/3 c. shortening
4 t. milk
1 t. vanilla extract

2 eggs
3-2/3 c. all-purpose flour
2-1/2 t. baking powder
1/2 t. salt

Mix sugar, shortening, milk, vanilla and eggs together. Add flour, baking powder and salt. Divide dough in half, wrap and chill at least one hour. Roll out and cut into 2-inch rounds with cutter or glass. Place bottom rounds on cookie sheet, fill with 1/4 teaspoon date filling, top with second rounds and press edges together with a fork. Bake at 400 degrees for 8 to 10 minutes, or until slightly brown.

Date Filling:

1 T. all-purpose flour
1/2 c. sugar

1 c. dates, finely chopped
1/2 c. water

In a medium pan, mix flour with sugar; stir in dates and water. Cook over low heat, stirring constantly, until mixture thickens.

Host a tea party for your friends! Serve a variety of flavored teas and cookies. Ask each guest to bring her own tea cup; it's fun to see the different patterns.

Pineapple-Nut Cookies

Norma Longnecker
Lawrenceville, IL

I've enjoyed these cookies for years. I began making them when my children were small, and now I make them for my grandkids.

1/2 c. butter
1/2 t. vanilla extract
1 c. brown sugar, packed
1 egg
1/2 t. salt

1 t. baking soda
1/2 c. pecans, chopped
3/4 c. crushed pineapple
2-1/2 c. all-purpose flour

Mix all ingredients together and drop by spoonfuls onto an ungreased cookie sheet. Bake in a 375 degree oven for 10 to 12 minutes.

Mystery Bars

Shirley Hudson
Spokane, WA

These taste just like toffee...yum!

1 c. butter
1 c. brown sugar, packed
40 saltine crackers

2 c. semi-sweet chocolate chips
1 to 2 c. walnuts, finely ground

Boil butter and brown sugar in a saucepan for 3 minutes. Arrange the 40 crackers on a cookie sheet, lined up against each other, not overlapping. Spread the butter and sugar mixture over the crackers. Bake at 350 degrees for 5 minutes. Take them out of the oven and pour the chocolate chips on top immediately. When the chips melt, spread out the chocolate evenly. Sprinkle with the ground walnuts. Place the cookie sheet into the fridge to cool. Cut or break bars.

When I give, I give myself.

-Walt Whitman

Praline Shortbread Cookies

Carol Hickman
Kingsport, TN

It just isn't Christmas at our house without these cookies!

1-1/2 c. butter, softened and
   divided
3 c. powdered sugar, divided
2 c. all-purpose flour
1 c. pecans, finely chopped

1 T. plus 1/2 t. vanilla extract,
   divided
1 c. brown sugar, packed
1/8 t. salt
1/2 c. evaporated milk

Cream together one cup butter and one cup powdered sugar. Add flour, stirring until well blended. Stir in pecans and one tablespoon vanilla. Shape into one-inch balls and place 2 inches apart on ungreased cookie sheets. Make an indentation in center of each cookie. Bake at 375 degrees for 15 minutes; do not brown. Cool on wire racks. In saucepan, melt remaining butter. Add brown sugar and salt; bring to a boil for 2 minutes, stirring constantly. Remove from heat, stir in evaporated milk, then return to heat. Once again, bring to a boil for 2 minutes. Remove from heat and allow mixture to cool to lukewarm. Stir in remaining powdered sugar and vanilla with a wooden spoon; stirring until smooth. Fill indentations in cookies with praline filling. Makes about 3 dozen cookies.

Trace your favorite cookie cutters on colorful paper... hearts, stars, apples, gingerbread men; they'll make wonderful gift tags!

Cookie Jar Gingersnaps

Susan Kennedy
Delaware, OH

*These spicy cookies taste wonderful! They're great for a
holiday open house or cookie exchange.*

2 c. all-purpose flour
1 T. ginger
2 t. baking soda
1 t. cinnamon
1/2 t. salt

3/4 c. shortening
2 c. sugar, divided
1 egg
1/4 c. molasses

Sift together first 5 ingredients. Cream shortening and one cup sugar
gradually creaming until well blended. Beat in egg and molasses. Mix
in dry ingredients; form into small balls and roll in remaining sugar.
Place 2 inches apart on ungreased cookie sheet. Bake in a 350 degree
oven for 12 to 15 minutes or until tops are rounded, crackly and
lightly brown.

COME INTO MY KITCHEN
AND CHAT WITH ME
WHILE I PREPARE
A POT OF TEA.

*Cross stitch a small sampler for a friend. Lightly stuff and
stitch closed and it becomes a sweet gift tag when tied
on a basket or jar filled with homemade cookies.*

good
bt like other
better

Banana Cream Brownies

Marit Mentzer
Franklin, IN

If you're looking for a new treat; try these brownies. They'll remind you of a chocolate-covered banana!

15-oz. pkg. brownie mix
3/4 c. dry roasted peanuts, chopped and divided
2 bananas, sliced
5-1/4 oz. pkg. instant vanilla pudding mix

1-1/4 c. cold milk
8 oz. whipped topping, divided
Garnish: 1 oz. semi-sweet baking chocolate,
9 strawberries, sliced and
1 banana, sliced

Prepare brownie mix according to package directions; stir in 1/2 cup peanuts. Pour into 9"x9" pan and bake according to package directions; cool completely. Place 2/3 of banana slices in a single layer over brownie. In another bowl, whisk dry pudding into milk; beat until mixture just begins to thicken. Gently fold in 2-1/2 cups of whipped topping. Quickly spread pudding mixture over bananas. Refrigerate 30 minutes. Sprinkle remaining peanuts over pudding mixture. Use remaining topping for individual serving slices. Grate chocolate over dessert and garnish each slice with banana and strawberry slices.

Use mini cookie cutters to make whimsical vents for steam on your top pie crust. Oak or maple leaves for fall, stars for Independence day or tiny trees for Christmas!

Cookies & Brownies

Oatmeal & Toffee Cookies

Ramona Bowden
Hemet, CA

Toffee and pecans are a terrific, crunchy combination!

3/4 c. shortening
1-1/4 c. brown sugar, packed
1 egg
2 T. milk
1 t. vanilla extract
1/2 t. maple extract

2 c. quick-cooking oatmeal
1 c. all-purpose flour
1/2 t. baking soda
1/2 t. salt
1 c. toffee brickle chips, divided
1 c. pecans, coarsely chopped

Combine shortening, brown sugar, egg, milk, vanilla and maple extract in a large bowl. Using electric mixer, beat at medium speed until well blended. Combine oatmeal, flour, baking soda and salt. Mix into creamed mixture at low speed just until blended. Stir in 3/4 cup toffee chips and nuts. Form dough into 1-1/4 inch balls. Dip tops in remaining toffee chips. Place on greased baking sheets and flatten slightly with the back of a spoon. Bake at 375 degrees for 10 to 12 minutes or until cookies begin to brown around the edges. Cool for 2 minutes on baking sheet. Remove cookies to rack to cool completely. Makes 3 to 4 dozen.

Use a heart-in-hand cookie cutter to say thank you to a friend for lending a helping hand!

Nut Horns

Richard Welsch
Toledo, OH

*My wife's grandmother always made these for the holidays. I am
thrilled she shared the recipe so we can continue the delicious
tradition...thank you Grandma Lopuszynski!*

2 eggs, separated and divided
1 c. sour cream
4 c. all-purpose flour
1/2 lb. butter
1 t. salt

2 t. vanilla extract, divided
1 lb. walnuts, ground
1 c. sugar
2 T. lemon juice
Garnish: powdered sugar

Mix egg yolks with sour cream. In separate bowl, mix flour, butter,
salt and one teaspoon vanilla. Add sour cream and egg mixture
and mix until well blended. Shape into balls the size of a walnut;
refrigerate overnight. In separate bowl, blend walnuts, egg whites,
sugar, one teaspoon vanilla and lemon juice. Roll each ball into a circle
about 1/4-inch thick. Spread a heaping tablespoon of nut mixture onto
center of cookie. Roll dough circle into a log, then shape into a
horseshoe shape. Bake at 350 degrees for 30 minutes. When cool,
sprinkle with powdered sugar. Makes 50 cookies.

*Do you know someone who
loves to bake? Fill plastic
zipping bags with the dry
ingredients to your
favorite cookie recipe.
Tuck in a spatula, fun
cookie cutter, sprinkles
and your recipe!*

Sweet Nellie's Brownies

Shelly Taylor
Grand Junction, CO

A favorite brownie filled with double chocolate.

1/2 c. plus 1/3 c. margarine,
   softened and divided
2 c. sugar, divided
4 eggs
16-oz. can chocolate syrup
1 t. vanilla extract

1 c. all-purpose flour
1/2 t. salt
1/3 c. milk
2/3 c. semi-sweet chocolate
   chips
2/3 c. mini-marshmallows

In a mixing bowl, cream 1/2 cup margarine and one cup sugar. Add eggs, one at a time, beating well after each. Beat in chocolate syrup and vanilla. Add flour and salt, stirring until blended. Pour into a greased 15"x10" baking pan. Bake at 350 degrees for 20 to 25 minutes. Cool for 20 minutes on wire rack. In a small saucepan, combine remaining sugar, margarine and milk. Bring to a boil until sugar is dissolved. Remove from heat and stir in chocolate chips and marshmallows until melted. Pour over brownies and spread evenly. Allow glaze to set before cutting.

The road to a friend's house is never long.

-Old saying

Peanut Butter & Chip Cookies

Jackie Anderson
Deport, TX

At our house, these disappear from the cooling rack!

2 eggs
1/3 c. water
1/4 c. margarine, melted
1-1/2 c. peanut butter

1-1/2 c. brown sugar, packed
18-1/4 oz. yellow cake mix,
    divided
12-oz. pkg. chocolate chips

Beat together eggs, water, margarine, peanut butter, brown sugar and half the dry cake mix until smooth. Stir in remaining cake mix with chocolate chips. Drop by rounded teaspoonfuls onto ungreased cookie sheets. Bake at 375 degrees for 10 minutes.

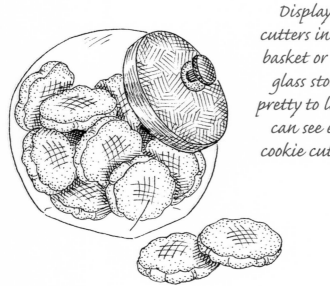

Display your cookie cutters in a handwoven basket or old-fashioned glass storage jar...so pretty to look at and you can see exactly what cookie cutters you have!

Licorice Snaps

Eleanore Erickson
Griffith, IN

I have baked these cookies for 23 years at Franklin Elementary school in Griffith, Indiana. I still have fond memories of their aroma while baking and their delicious taste.

2-1/2 c. all-purpose flour
1 c. sugar
1 c. brown sugar, packed
1 t. baking soda
1/2 t. salt
1/2 t. cloves

1/2 t. cinnamon
1 c. butter
1 egg
1 T. anise seeds
1/2 c. pecans, chopped

Combine all ingredients in a large bowl; mix well. Divide dough in half and shape into two 10-inch long rolls. Wrap in wax paper; chill. Cut into 1/4-inch slices. Place on ungreased cookie sheet. Bake at 375 degrees for 10 to 12 minutes.

Button Cookies are a great way to say, "Sew glad we're friends!" Make your favorite sugar cookie dough recipe and cut out the cookies with a glass dipped in sugar. A drinking straw easily makes 2 holes in the center of each cookie, then bake according to your recipe.

Aunt Ruth's Brownie Bars

Denise Blaine
Sheppard AFB, TX

I love these served with a tall glass of milk!

1 c. butter
4 1-oz. squares unsweetened
   chocolate
2-1/2 c. sugar, divided
4 eggs, divided

2 t. vanilla extract, divided
1 c. all-purpose flour
1/2 t. salt
8-oz. pkg. cream cheese

In saucepan, over low heat, heat butter and chocolate until completely melted. In a bowl, add chocolate mixture and beat in 2 cups of sugar, 3 eggs and one teaspoon vanilla until blended. Stir in flour and salt. Spread in a greased 13"x9" pan and set aside. In a small bowl, with a mixer at low speed, beat cream cheese, remaining sugar, egg and vanilla until just mixed. Increase speed to medium and beat about 2 minutes until fully blended. Drop mixture by spoonfuls on top of brownie batter. Score the top surface in a criss-cross pattern. Bake at 350 degrees for 45 to 50 minutes or until a toothpick comes out clean. Cool on a wire rack then cut into bars. Best kept refrigerated.

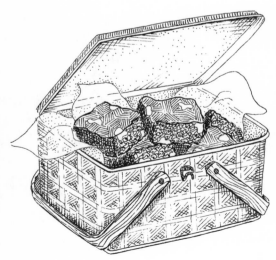

Surprise a teacher with an apple filled lunch box! Tuck in apple-shaped sugar cookies, apple bars and thumbprint cookies filled with apple jelly.

Triple Chippers

Kim Duffy
Sheridan, IL

Tasty, chunky cookies filled with three favorite flavors!

1 c. butter
1 c. sugar
1 c. brown sugar, packed
2 eggs
1 t. vanilla extract
2-1/2 c. quick cooking oatmeal
2 c. all-purpose flour

1 t. baking powder
1 t. baking soda
6-oz. pkg. peanut butter chips
6-oz. pkg. white chocolate chips
6-oz. pkg. chocolate chips
1-1/2 c. walnuts, chopped

Cream together butter and sugars. Add eggs and vanilla. Using a blender or food processor, process the oatmeal until it turns to powder. In a separate bowl, mix the oatmeal, flour, baking powder and baking soda. Add peanut butter chips, white chocolate chips, chocolate chips and walnuts, stir into egg mixture. Drop by tablespoonfuls, 2 inches apart, onto an ungreased baking sheet. Bake at 375 degrees for about 7 minutes.

Layered cookie and brownie mixes are so easy to make and such fun to receive! Make each gift a little different...tie on a wooden spoon, cookie cutter, wire whisk or set of measuring spoons.

Cinnamon Cheesecake Squares

Cindy Elser
Naples, FL

Sweet and spicy; try serving with a scoop of cinnamon ice cream.

2 8-oz. tubes refrigerated
   crescent rolls
2 8-oz. pkgs. cream cheese

1-1/2 c. sugar, divided
2 T. cinnamon
1 stick butter, melted

Spread one tube of crescent rolls in bottom of an ungreased
13"x9" pan. Mix cream cheese and one cup sugar; spread over rolls.
Layer the second tube of crescent rolls over cream cheese mixture.
Combine remaining sugar and cinnamon; sprinkle over the top, drizzle
with butter. Bake at 350 degrees for 25 minutes.

Mom's Monster Cookies

Susie Backus
Gooseberry Patch

Packed with lots of yummy favorites!

6 eggs
2 sticks margarine
1 lb. brown sugar
2 c. sugar
1/8 c. vanilla extract
6 T. corn syrup
1-1/2 lbs. peanut butter

4 t. baking soda
9 c. quick-cooking oatmeal
1/2 lb. chocolate chips
1/2 lb. peanuts
1/2 lb. candy-coated chocolate
   pieces

In a large bowl, mix ingredients in order listed. Drop by rounded
teaspoonfuls onto an ungreased cookie sheet. Bake at 350 degrees for
15 to 20 minutes. Makes 12 dozen cookies.

Pile cookie cutters and rolling pins in an old wooden
bowl or basket... you'll be ready to bake anytime.

Cookies & Brownies

NOT Really!

Cappuccino Brownies

Robin Paterson
Roseburg, OR

If you love the blend of coffee and chocolate, give these a try!

4 1-oz. squares unsweetened
   chocolate, melted
3/4 c. butter, melted
2 c. sugar
5 eggs, divided
1 t. vanilla extract
3 T. instant coffee granules

1-1/4 c. plus 2 T. all-purpose
   flour, divided
8-oz. pkg. cream cheese,
   softened
1/3 c. sugar
1/2 t. cinnamon

Place chocolate and butter into a large bowl; stir in 2 cups sugar until
well blended. Mix in 4 eggs, vanilla and coffee. Stir in 1-1/4 cups flour
until combined. Spread in a greased, foil-lined 13"x9" baking pan.
Beat cream cheese, sugar, remaining egg, flour and cinnamon in same
bowl until well blended. Spoon mixture over brownie batter and swirl
with a knife to marble top. Bake at 350 degrees for 40 minutes or
until toothpick inserted in center comes out with fudgy crumbs. Cool
in pan. Cut into squares. Makes 24 brownies.

*Sending a care package to a student
away at school? Spell out their college
letters on homemade cookies!
Roll dough in a circle and lay a letter
stencil on top. Use a toothpick to
prick holes along the inside opening of
the stencil, then use a sharp knife to
trace around the outside of the
stencil. Lift off stencil, repeat with
remaining dough then bake
according to the recipe.*

Country Kitchen Sugar Cookies

Michel Johnson
Woodinville, WA

A recipe shared with me 27 years ago when I was a new bride just beginning to collect recipes; it quickly became a favorite.

1 c. powdered sugar	1 t. cream of tartar
1 c. sugar	1 t. baking soda
1 c. margarine	1 t. salt
1 c. oil	4-1/4 c. all-purpose flour
2 eggs	1 t. vanilla extract

Mix sugars, margarine, oil and eggs together. Add dry ingredients and vanilla. Refrigerate until firm. Roll dough into balls and flatten with a glass that has been dipped in sugar. Bake at 350 degrees for approximately 8 minutes or until edges are slightly brown. Cookies will spread while baking, so do not make dough balls too large. Cool slightly on cookie sheet and then remove to rack to cool completely.

Turn your favorite quilt pattern into a potholder.
Stitch together a quilt block, add a pocket in the back.
Slip in recipe cards of all your best-loved recipes.
Great for a college student!

Great Grandma Ownie's Cookies

Kerry Varner
Keokuk, IA

I still remember the first time I enjoyed these cookies warm from the oven...they immediately became my favorite.

1-1/2 c. brown sugar, packed
3/4 c. shortening
2 eggs
1 t. vanilla extract
1 t. orange zest
1/2 c. buttermilk

1/2 t. baking soda
1/2 t. salt
1-1/2 t. baking powder
2-1/2 c. all-purpose flour
1/3 c. orange juice
1 c. sugar

In large bowl, mix together brown sugar, shortening, eggs, vanilla, zest and buttermilk. Add baking soda, salt, baking powder and flour. Drop by teaspoonfuls onto an ungreased baking sheet. Bake at 350 degrees for 10 minutes or until golden brown. In a saucepan, heat orange juice and sugar. When sugar is melted, spoon some of the juice mixture onto cookies while they cool.

A fun gift for a country friend... spotted cow cookies! Roll out your favorite sugar cookie dough; cut out. Frost with white icing, then place black icing in a pastry bag. Using a small tip, draw spots on the white cookies.

Grandma Bletso's Fruit Cookies

Diane Long
Delaware, OH

This recipe was handed down from my husband's Grandma Bletso, who lived to be 101. She always did all her own baking and these cookies became a holiday treat.

1 c. butter	3 eggs
1-1/2 c. brown sugar, packed	1 c. raisins
1/2 t. salt	1/2 c. molasses
1 t. cloves	3-1/2 c. all-purpose flour
1 t. cinnamon	1 t. baking soda
1 t. allspice	1 c. walnuts, chopped

Cream butter, brown sugar and salt together; add spices. Add eggs, one at a time, mixing well after each addition. Stir in raisins and add molasses. Add flour and soda together. Stir in nuts and blend into egg mixture. Dough will be stiff. Drop by spoonfuls on well greased baking sheets. Slightly flatten them leaving a space between as the cookies will spread. Bake in a 350 degree oven for 8 to 10 minutes.

Whimsical cookie cutters can be used to make patterns to stitch simple ornaments. . . hearts, stars or bells.

Apple-Date Dream Squares

Ruth Cooksey
Plainfield, IN

I'm known as the "recipe lady" in our town;
I've shared my recipes with everyone!

2 c. all-purpose flour	2 eggs, beaten
1 c. sugar	14-1/2 oz. can apple pie filling
1 t. salt	1/2 c. oil
1-1/2 t. baking soda	1 t. vanilla extract
1 t. cinnamon	1/2 c. pecans, chopped
1/2 t. allspice	1 c. dates, chopped

Sift together flour, sugar, salt, baking soda, cinnamon and allspice. Stir in eggs, pie filling, oil, vanilla, pecans and dates. Pour into a greased 13"x9" pan. Bake at 325 degrees for 40 to 45 minutes. When cool, cut into squares.

Aunt Glo's Best Brownies

Mary Pargett
Syracuse, NE

Every time our family visited Aunt Glo she always
had a plate of these brownies waiting for us.

1 c. margarine	2 t. vanilla extract
2 c. sugar	4 eggs
1-1/2 c. all-purpose flour	1 c. chocolate chips
1/2 c. cocoa	Garnish: powdered sugar

Melt margarine in a large bowl in the microwave. Blend in all other ingredients. Bake at 350 degrees in a greased and floured 13"x9" pan for 25 minutes. Dust with powdered sugar while still warm.

Ah, how good it feels! The hand of an old friend!

-Henry Wadsworth Longfellow

Thumbprint Cookies

*Calico Inn
Sevierville, TN*

Fill these yummy cookies with your favorite flavor of jam or jelly!

1/2 c. butter
3 T. powdered sugar
1 t. vanilla extract
1 c. all-purpose flour

1 c. nuts, finely chopped
8-oz. jar strawberry jelly
Garnish: powdered sugar

Cream butter and sugar; stir in vanilla. Add dry ingredients a little at a time until mixed; chill overnight. Roll dough into equal size balls. Place thumbprint in the middle of each, flattening slightly, and fill with jelly. Bake at 375 degrees on an ungreased cookie sheet for 15 minutes or until golden. Sprinkle with powdered sugar when cooled. Makes one dozen.

*Tiny thumbprints! Have the little ones make
thumbprint cookies for Grandma & Grandpa.
Send them along with recent family photos, notes from
the kids or even a videotape. . . a memorable gift!*

Chocolate-Raspberry Brownies

Susan Brzozowski
Ellicott City, MD

The layer of raspberries make these brownies really special.

1 c. unsalted butter
5 oz. unsweetened chocolate, chopped
2 c. sugar
4 eggs
2 t. vanilla extract

1-1/4 c. all-purpose flour
1 t. baking powder
1/2 t. salt
1 c. walnuts, toasted and chopped
1/2 c. raspberry preserves

Melt butter and chocolate in heavy saucepan over low heat, stirring constantly until smooth. Remove from heat. Whisk in sugar, eggs and vanilla. Mix flour, baking powder and salt in a small bowl. Add to chocolate mixture and whisk to blend. Stir in nuts. Pour 2 cups batter into a buttered 13"x9" pan. Freeze until firm, about 10 minutes. Spread preserves over frozen brownie batter in pan, spoon remaining batter over preserves. Let stand 20 minutes at room temperature to thaw. Bake brownies at 350 degrees for approximately 35 minutes, or until tester comes out clean. Transfer to rack to cool. Makes about 2 dozen brownies.

Having a cookie exchange? Display your cookies in creative ways...on tiered cake stands, tucked inside painted clay pots, dough bowls, vintage cookie jars, nostalgic hatboxes, painted tins or layered in a tall glass trifle bowl.

Blueberry Crumb Bars

good like muffins w/toppin'

Kim Olsen
Bridgeport, CT

You could easily substitute blackberries or mulberries if you'd like, but blueberry always seems to be our favorite flavor!

1 c. plus 1/2 c. sugar, divided
3 c. all-purpose flour
1 t. baking powder
1 c. shortening
1 egg

1/8 t. salt
1/8 t. cinnamon
4 c. blueberries
3 t. cornstarch

Mix together one cup sugar, flour, baking powder, shortening, egg, salt and cinnamon. Mix well with pastry cutter or fork; dough will be crumbly. Pat half of the dough into a greased 13"x9" pan. Mix together blueberries, remaining sugar and cornstarch. Place mixture into pan over dough. Crumble remaining dough over berries. Bake at 375 degrees for 45 minutes or until top is slightly brown. Makes 12 to 15 bars.

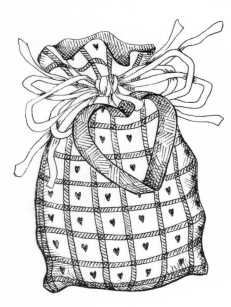

Share your blueberry crumb bars! Fill a one-quart zipping bag with the dry ingredients; seal. Stitch homespun fabric into a 12"x6" bag and tuck your one-quart bag inside; tie closed with raffia. Give with the recipe and a basket of fresh blueberries from the farmers' market!

Austrian Raspberry Bars

Susan Gurley
St. Charles, MO

*I keep different flavors of jam on hand so if friends
drop by I can make this treat quickly.*

1 c. butter	1 t. vanilla extract
1 c. sugar	2 c. all-purpose flour
2 egg yolks	1-1/2 c. raspberry jam

Cream together butter and sugar. Add egg yolks, vanilla and flour. Mix together well. Pat about 2/3 of the dough in the bottom of an ungreased 13"x9" pan. Spread jam on top of dough. Crumble remaining dough on top of jam. Bake at 350 degrees for 25 minutes.

Peanut Butter Cookies

Cindy Pogge
Kanawha, IA

*Who doesn't love peanut butter and chocolate together?
Here's a twist on a familiar cookie we think you'll love.*

1 c. all-purpose flour	1 c. peanut butter
1 t. baking soda	1/2 c. butter
1/8 t. salt	1 egg
1/2 c. brown sugar, packed	1/2 t. vanilla extract
1/4 c. sugar	8-oz. pkg. chocolate star candies

Sift flour, baking soda and salt together. In a large bowl, cream together sugars, peanut butter, butter, egg and vanilla. Combine the dry ingredients with the cream mixture until well blended. Refrigerate at least one hour. Roll into one-inch balls and bake in a 375 degree oven for 10 to 12 minutes. Remove from the oven and place a chocolate star in the center of each cookie. Cool completely on a wire rack until the chocolate has set.

That's the way the cookie crumbles!

-Old saying

Whoopie Pies

Karen Slack
Mt. Pleasant, TX

*When I was a school secretary, a student always brought these
to me and they quickly became a favorite.*

2-1/4 c. plus 5 t. all-purpose
    flour, divided
1/2 c. cocoa
1-1/2 t. baking soda
1-1/4 c. sugar
1-1/4 t. cream of tartar
1-2/3 c. shortening, divided

2 c. milk, divided
2 eggs
1 T. plus 1 t. vanilla extract,
    divided
1/2 c. butter
1 c. powdered sugar
1/4 t. salt

Mix 2-1/4 cups flour, cocoa, baking soda, sugar, cream of tartar,
2/3 cup shortening, one cup milk, eggs and one teaspoon vanilla
together. Drop by teaspoonfuls onto greased cookie sheet. Bake at
300 degrees for 15 minutes. In a saucepan, cook remaining milk and
flour until thick; cool. Blend together with remaining ingredients until
fluffy. Spread between 2 cooled cookies. Wrap in plastic wrap; chill.
Makes 2 dozen.

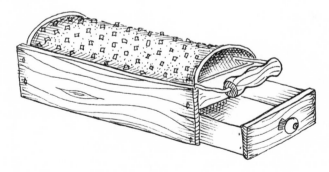

*Let kids decorate cookies with edible cookie paint!
You'll need one egg yolk for each color of "paint." Drop egg yolks
into separate bowls, stir with a fork and add 1/4 teaspoon
of different food coloring to each yolk; mix well. Brush paint
on cookies then bake according to recipe.*

Chocolate Chip-Raisin Cookies

Judy Borecky
Escondido, CA

Sometimes I add extra chocolate chips instead of raisins, or you could use peanut butter or butterscotch chips, too.

1 c. margarine, softened
1 c. shortening
2 c. sugar
2 c. brown sugar, packed
2 t. vanilla extract
4 eggs
4 c. all-purpose flour

2 t. baking soda
2 t. salt
3-1/2 c. quick-cooking oatmeal
2 c. walnuts, chopped
2 c. chocolate chips
2 c. raisins

Cream margarine, shortening, sugars and vanilla. Add eggs, blending well. Stir in dry ingredients just until blended. Add nuts, chocolate chips and raisins. Drop on ungreased cookie sheets and bake at 375 degrees until golden brown, about 12 to 14 minutes.

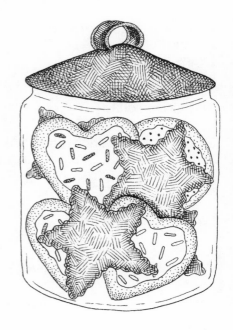

You may talk about your vases,
Just how beautiful they are,
but to me there's nothing nicer,
than a well-filled cookie jar.

-Elsie Duncan Yale

Grandmother's Oatmeal Bars

Dixie Sorensen
Exira, IA

Topped with a tasty chocolate and peanut butter icing!

4 c. quick-cooking oatmeal
1/2 c. corn syrup
2 t. vanilla extract
1 c. brown sugar, packed

2/3 c. butter, melted
12-oz. pkg. chocolate chips
2/3 c. peanut butter

Mix oatmeal, corn syrup, vanilla, brown sugar and butter. Place in a lightly oiled 13"x9" pan. Bake 10 to 15 minutes at 350 degrees. Heat together chocolate chips and peanut butter; spread on cooled bars.

Honey & Spice Cookies

Donna Fish
American Canyon, CA

You can form the balls then freeze if you're planning ahead. Just thaw, dip in sugar and bake.

4 c. brown sugar, packed
3 c. shortening
4 eggs
1 c. honey
9 c. all-purpose flour
6 t. baking soda

2 t. salt
4 t. ginger
3 t. cinnamon
1 t. cloves
Garnish: sugar

Cream sugar and shortening; add eggs and honey. Add dry ingredients and roll into balls. Dip into water then into sugar. Bake at 350 degrees for 10 to 12 minutes.

The best way to cheer yourself up is to cheer someone else up.

-Mark Twain

Wild Blueberry Gingerbread

Gail Hageman
Albion, ME

Because it's a twist on an old favorite, this gingerbread is always popular when I take it to a potluck dinner.

1 c. sugar	2-1/2 c. all-purpose flour
1/2 t. cloves	1/2 c. molasses
1/2 t. cinnamon	2 eggs
1/2 t. ginger	1/2 c. oil
1 t. salt	1 c. hot tea
1 t. baking soda	1 c. blueberries

Mix together first 7 ingredients. Add molasses, eggs, oil and tea. Carefully fold in blueberries. Pour batter into greased and floured 13"x9" pan. Bake at 350 degrees for about 35 minutes.

Make stained glass cookies for a special occasion. Roll out cookie dough and cut with cookie cutters. Use a mini cookie cutter to cut out the center. Place cookies on cookie sheet and fill center with crushed fruit-flavored candies. Bake according to recipe directions or until candy is melted.

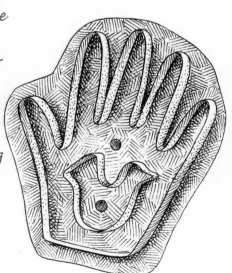

Surprise Cookies

Francie Stutzman
Dalton, OH

The surprise is a minty chocolate center...yum!

1 c. butter	3 c. all-purpose flour
1 c. sugar	1 t. baking soda
1/2 c. brown sugar, packed	1/2 t. salt
2 eggs	24 chocolate mint wafers
1 t. vanilla extract	24 walnut halves

Cream butter, sugar and brown sugar together. Beat in eggs and vanilla. Sift the dry ingredients together and add to butter mixture. Drop by spoonfuls onto an ungreased cookie sheet. Press a chocolate mint wafer in the center of each cookie, cover with another spoonful of dough and top with a walnut half. Bake at 350 degrees for 10 to 12 minutes. Makes about 2 dozen cookies.

Keep jars of homebaked goodies on your pantry shelf.
They're a handy gift if you're expecting guests
or for late night snacking!

Cookies & Brownies

Hucklebucks

Shannon Ellis
Mount Vernon, WA

Soft chocolate cookies with a marshmallow filling.

3/4 c. shortening
2 eggs
3/4 c. cocoa
3 t. vanilla extract, divided
1-1/2 c. sugar
3 c. all-purpose flour

3 t. baking powder
3/4 t. plus 1/8 t. salt, divided
1-1/2 c. plus 1 T. milk, divided
3/4 c. butter
2 c. powdered sugar
1 c. marshmallow creme

Cream together shortening, eggs, cocoa, 1-1/2 teaspoons vanilla and sugar. Sift together flour, baking powder and 3/4 teaspoon salt. Add 1-1/2 cups milk to cocoa mixture alternating with dry ingredients. Mix well after each addition until batter is smooth. Drop by tablespoonfuls onto ungreased baking sheets. Bake at 400 degrees for 7 to 8 minutes; cool. Blend together remaining ingredients; spread on one side of a cookie and top with a second cookie. Repeat with remaining cookies and store in an air-tight container.

When you meet someone who can cook and do housework, don't hesitate a minute... marry him!

-Joy Adams

Index

Index

Index

"We would make. . . muffins for church suppers and deliver them in our buggy, drawn by Rebecca, our dun-colored mare. It was an event to drive to the supper. . . the wood thrushes would be singing as the sun set. It is a happy remembrance."

-Tasha Tudor

We've cooked up a whole collection of Gooseberry Patch® books!

Have a taste for more? Call us toll-free at

1-800-854-6673

We'll send you our latest catalog filled with kitchenware, candles, handmade quilts, gourmet goodies, enamelware, bowls, bubble night lights and our very own line of cookbooks, calendars and organizers!

Phone us:
1·800·854·6673

Fax us:
1·740·363·7225

Visit our website:
gooseberrypatch.com

Send us your favorite recipe!

and the memory that makes it special for you!* If we select your recipe for a brand new **Gooseberry Patch** cookbook, your name will appear right along with it...and you'll receive a FREE copy of the book! Mail to:

Vickie & Jo Ann
Gooseberry Patch, Dept. Book
600 London Road
Delaware, Ohio 43015

*Please include the number of servings and all other necessary information!

melt in your mouth chocolate chips ginge

served warm

freshly-baked bread

cinnamon rolls

birthday cakes

apple pies

smiles friendship cookie cutters ...odles